# the
# new
# sexuality

# the new sexuality

DR. HENDRIK M. RUITENBEEK

NEW VIEWPOINTS
A Division of Franklin Watts, Inc.
New York
1974

**Library of Congress Cataloging in Publication Data**

Ruitenbeek, Hendrik Marinus, 1928–
  The new sexuality.

  Includes bibliographical references.
  1. Sex.   2. Sex (Psychology)   3. Sexual
deviation.   I. Title.   [DNLM:   1. Sex—History.
2. Sex behavior.   HQ21 R934n 1975]
HQ21.R915       155.3       74–6399
ISBN 0-531-05360-1
ISBN 0-531-05565-5 (pbk.)

for Dr. Richard McConchie

*Whatever view we hold, it must be shown*
*Why every lover has a wish to make*
*Some other kind of otherness his own:*
*Perhaps, in fact, we never are alone.*

W. H. Auden, "Alone"


*L'énigme de la sexualité c'est qu'elle*
*reste irréductible a la trilogie qui fait*
*l'homme: langage-outil-institution.*

Paul Ricoeur in "Merveille, Errance, Enigme."

Preface                                                          ix
Foreword                                                         xi
Introduction                                                      1

PART 1: SEXUALITY IN ITS HISTORICAL CONTEXT
1   The Way of all Flesh                                          9
2   The German Sexologists and Their Empire                      16
3   The Lonely Englishman: Havelock Ellis                        30
4   Freud and Sexuality                                          42
5   The New Sexologists                                          55

PART 2: THE VARIETIES OF SEXUALITY
6   The Origins of Sexuality                                     67
7   The Myth of Bisexuality                                      75
8   Homosexuality: A Contemporary View                           82
9   Fetishism: Heterosexual and Homosexual                      101
10  Reflections on de Sade and Sadomasochism                    112

PART 3: SEXUALITY TODAY
11  Children, Parents, and Sexuality                            119
12  The Mass-Media Role in the Approach to Sexuality            132
13  Perspective on Sexuality in a Mass Society                  139
Notes                                                           147
Index                                                           159

# contents

Conceived many years ago, this book is the product of long and hard thinking about human sexuality. The current openness about and preoccupation with sexuality has not always produced the most scholarly works on the subject. Contemporary sexologists are often too tempted to give in to the sensational aspects of the study of human sexuality. I certainly do not pretend this to be a scholarly work in the tradition of Hirschfeld and Krafft-Ebing, but I have tried to present contemporary human sexuality in a more existential context.

I discussed at length with my associate Dr. Richard McConchie some of the historical parts of this book, and I owe him thanks for his contributions to my research and writing.


New York
Paris                                        Dr. Hendrik M. Ruitenbeek

This is a book on sexuality but not on sexuality only. I have tried to put sexuality into something of a historical context and then moved on to discuss some varieties of sexual behavior and to comment on the general state of sexuality in our society today.

Although many clinical observations are made, I have tried to avoid a merely clinical approach to sexuality, since I believe that cultural conditioning accounts for a large part of the distinctive character that sexuality assumes in any moment of historic time. As nations are said to have the rulers they deserve, so periods of history have the patterns of sexuality that their mores have earned for them.

Among the variations of sexuality I have emphasized bisexuality, homosexuality, fetishism, and sadomasochism, since these I think are not only fairly prevalent in contemporary culture, but are also related to its distinctive characteristics. Other manifestations of sexual expression such as transsexuality, transvestism, and exhibitionism should be dealt with in a more clinical context; these phenomena are disturbances of sexuality as much as they are expressions of the sexual impulse as shaped by the time in which they appear.

My approach to sexuality is primarily existential. Naturally, therefore, this book owes much to the work of Ricoeur, Boss, and Binswanger. In dealing with certain aspects of sexuality, however, I probably have gone beyond the strict psychoanalytic-existential approach; for that, of course, I carry the sole responsibility.

foreword

It is now clear that Freud and Kinsey have moved sex from the sanctum of the bedroom out into the open world of a questioning society. This shift and its consequences have, to a large degree, fundamentally changed our notions about sexuality. Sex is no longer set apart. Secrecy is rapidly disappearing, and we have begun to realize that few secrets are left in the realm of sexuality. In fact, nearly all the secrets of sexual behavior have been discovered and experienced. The literature on sexuality is growing fast. We are not interested merely in the sexuality of the past; [1] we are also curious about the present condition of our sexuality. [2] Sexuality now is not only traditional heterosexuality; the term covers all the areas of sexual experience.

If most people once considered their sexuality as a separate entity, not to be discussed, often not even realized and/or experienced, today few people fail to realize that sexuality cannot be denied. And in their continuous confrontation with society people now know that sexuality must be recognized and given its place. Repression is declining, and the here-and-now experience of sexuality is being stressed.

This by no means implies that our contemporaries enjoy total freedom of experience in terms of their sexuality. The impact of the Victorian [3] and puritanical past is still being felt—mostly in the realm of sexuality. The boundaries of sexual freedom, and for that matter of

# introduction

"For us, there is only the trying.
The rest is not our business."

T. S. Eliot, *Four Quartets*

sexuality *per se,* have not yet been fully defined. (Indeed, one might question whether such boundaries should be defined at all.)

Probably Freud's most important contribution to human civilization was the recognition that sexuality is a driving force within all of us, whether we face it or not. It can no longer be contained within the narrow confines of love and romanticism. In the modern context, eroticism and sexuality have become separate entities, much to the dismay of the moralizers in our society. Neither can it be disguised and couched in vague terms. Honesty is now a requirement for a confrontation with sexuality in our culture. Admittedly, many still cannot deal existentially with such a sexuality-in-the-world. Many may refuse to face the facts of the *new* sexuality, but they cannot change the outcome of a historical development.

For some decades now we have been talking about the sexual revolution, but this revolution in the final analysis means nothing other than a slow recognition that sexuality is part of our being and identity. The perversion of sexuality, that is, the distortions of sexuality by a puritanical society, has been our worst hindrance in defining sexuality in our contemporary situation. Not that there have not been pioneers in fighting the hypocritical sexual morality, which so hampered the development of an open and spontaneous sexuality,[4] but hypocrisy on sexual matters is still with us. A hypocrisy well expressed by that old roué King Leopold I, who in his time (around the 1830s) was known to have many mistresses, but who admonished his prim and proper wife, Queen Louise, when she cracked an innocent joke in public, by saying, ''No frivolous remarks, madam!'' [5]

Contemporary sexuality then has only one slogan: freedom, the freedom to experience *all* aspects of sexuality without restrictions. The Dutch writer J. J. Beljon has defined our situation in the following terms: ''The change in eroticism which we experience today has been conditioned by the fall of Christian morality. The act of intercourse no longer carries with it the taste of the forbidden fruit, since the peeping

Tom of Nazareth on his cross no longer hangs above the marital bed. Freedom has arrived. Freedom to love but also freedom to *Schund*. Freedom for great passion, but also freedom for *Unfug*. Freedom for fidelity, but also freedom for promiscuity. Henry Miller does not have to be bought under the counter, and neither does Genet or Burroughs. There is freedom for poetic game and sadomasochism, freedom for eros and freedom for necrophilia. Freedom is granted to the light, but also freedom is given to the shadows.'' [6]

The integration of sexuality into a person's identity cannot then be restricted to preconceived notions about what constitutes sexuality. This book does not deal with the overall problem of morality and abnormality in sexuality, for we have come to realize that these terms do not work for our confrontation with sexuality. Although I personally do not favor a socialization of sexuality in all its aspects as Ullerstam proposes in his book *The Erotic Minorities*, [7] I can see that we are moving toward a situation where no restrictions on sexuality are imposed upon those who want to experience it to its fullest.

The dimensions of sexuality have been enlarged just because we are willing and able to see it as part of our total experience in the world. So many of the distortions of sexuality in the past can be attributed to the restrictions on and the repression of sexuality. The more we realize that sexuality is part of our identity, the more we will be able to see sexuality as a functioning part of that identity.

The introduction of an *overt* sexuality into our culture and our awareness of that sexuality has had far-reaching consequences for our approaches to the sexual side of existence. We now realize (thanks to Freud) that sexuality and its symbols pervade our whole mode of life. Contemporary art and fashion alike acknowledge strong sexual aspects. The place of sexuality in these fields can no longer be denied. The fetish, heretofore an expression of perverse sexuality, has become an important element in today's fashion and fashionable art. [8] The forcing of sexuality into the open has accelerated our recognition of its significance and our identity and sense of self has been affected by the larger role that sexuality plays in our culture today.

Sexuality then becomes not only an important force in the rapidly changing picture of convention and tradition in matters of marriage, but also in the larger picture of sexual behavior, such as homosexuality and extramarital relations.

It is only during the last decades that we have been studying sexuality *in depth*. The latter part of the nineteenth century and the beginning of the twentieth century still witnessed an approach to sexuality that concerned itself with classifications rather than interpretations. Freud's *Three Contributions to Sexuality* was the first major breakthrough in the interpretation of sexuality, and it has been a major contribution of classical psychoanalysis to have gone even beyond mere classification. For regardless of Kinsey *et al.*, we are still at the beginning of the study of all aspects of sexuality. Too often we are still caught in the moralizing attitudes of a post-Victorian and puritanical society. Unless we begin to separate the question of morality (not ethics) from study and research concerning sexuality, we will not be able to achieve a significant and meaningful theory of that phenomenon. Many sexologists themselves are still burdened by their own prejudices and their lack of scientific objectivity.

The pressures that have been brought against the individual during the past decades have dramatized a crisis in identity, a crisis in terms of a man's relating to himself, to others, and to society at large. Obviously, such a crisis in identity also profoundly affects the sexual situation of a given individual. A man or woman in crisis about his or her place in society, family, and profession cannot escape doubts about his sexual identity. Moreover, sexual identities have been blurred by the demand of society for the individual to declare himself sexually. Today there is no way out for a person whose sexual identity might be confused. Society demands that he confront such a situation. Less sublimation, in other words, and more action!

The question of sexual identity is one of personal identity. The trouble in our contemporary culture is that the disintegration of personal identities has been closely linked to sexuality. In no society is there such insecurity about concepts of femininity and masculinity.[9] Men are tortured by the very thought of not being considered virile; their sexuality seems much more in peril than that of contemporary women, who still seem to be able to hold on to established concepts of femininity.

Sexuality then has become much more fluid, the lines between the aggressiveness of men and the passivity of women are disintegrating. Contemporary patients are more than ever concerned about their sexual roles and are increasingly unable to define for themselves a mode of behavior. Since established notions about sexuality have been shattered,[10] many men and women look for guidelines on how to deal with their sexuality. Everyone is only too willing today to discuss sexual tastes and behavior. There is an openness about sexuality, which is encouraging, but at the same time few persons take the responsibility for their choice. Then, too, sexuality has become another commodity in our culture, and one sometimes wonders at the apparent ease with which people talk about their choice of sexuality, as if they could buy masculinity or femininity at the neighborhood supermarket. Part of this attitude stems from a feeling of being left out, or even more, of having missed something![11]

In the overall position of sexuality in our culture we are still plagued by the notion of sexuality as a separate entity, divorced from one's whole life situation. It must be reiterated that the behavior of a person cannot be separated from the way he functions in his sexual situation. Of course, in a society where personal sexual bias is still rather strong, such a situation has not yet been reached.

Further, one must realize that many have not freed themselves from guilt and preconceived notions about sex, because many of the churches are still caught up in long outdated concepts of sexuality.[12]

The blending of personal and sexual identities in this culture in the years to come will depend mainly on how we cope with the increasing anomie and alienation in our personal lives; it will depend on how we deal with the increasing impact of technology on our lives. The danger of desexualization [13] as a result of a robot society is not to be dismissed lightly. The separation between feeling and sexuality is already with us in many ways. In the confrontation between identity and a technological society, the question of sexuality cannot any longer be ignored.

**part 1** SEXUALITY IN ITS
HISTORICAL CONTEXT

On November 20, 1900, English poet, playwright, and social light Oscar Wilde died in a small room in the Hotel d'Alsace Rue des Beaux-Arts in Paris. With what was left of his strength, he protested against the horrible wallpaper of his small, tacky room. He died of alcoholism, but the true cause of the disaster met by this enchanter of the London beau monde was not absinthe but his trial three years before for *unnatural sexual behavior*. He was convicted and sentenced to two years of forced labor in prison. The trial of Oscar Wilde brought into the social spotlight the conflict between two versions of sexual morality: The old morality based itself firmly on Christianity; the new morality stressed the responsibility of man toward man, rather than toward God, and at the same time, it rejected the whole concept of sin as the ethical center of sexual behavior.

In looking closely at the old morality one sees that it never fully dominated sexual life. The temptation to violate the Bible's sexual prohibitions was much stronger than the temptation to break the commandment "Thou shalt not kill." The nineteenth century, particularly, developed a dual morality. In the first place, there was the double standard: Men were allowed a much more independent sexual life than women. Their sexual needs were recognized and society allowed men to meet those needs outside the bonds of marriage. Prostitution has generally been

THE WAY OF
ALL FLESH

recognized as an offense; that men resorted to prostitutes was considered sinful, but the sin seemed unavoidable and so was tolerated. Admittedly, neither the secular nor the religious authorities derived revenue from brothels in the nineteenth century as they had earlier, especially during the Middle Ages. Nevertheless, the Code Napoleon permitted *maisons de tolerance* to exist and even placed them under medical and police supervision, thus seeking to guarantee their patrons against assault or venereal infection. Prostitutes were looked on as degraded beings, but their male patrons were usually regarded as subject to mere human weakness, a minor weakness at that. When a man of respectable standing kept a mistress, that, too, was acceptable. But a married woman who took a lover—especially in England—lost her social standing if she were found out—unless, of course, the lover was a member of royalty. When a particularly successful prostitute rose to the level of courtesan and exhausted her patrons' fortunes to satisfy her extravagant demands, the men might well be regarded as unfortunate, but very few parents would refuse them as husbands for their daughters.

The second aspect of dual morality lay in the institution of marriage itself. Marrying for money was socially acceptable even where the convention of romantic love had taken root, but a woman who fell in love with a man other than her husband found it all but impossible to make any public acknowledgment of that love. Indeed, if it were expressed and that expression was discovered, the woman would lose her place in society. If her husband divorced her and she did marry her lover, she still was required to inhabit a kind of half world. Divorce and respectability were considered incompatible—even for men. Many a nineteenth-century political career was cut short by scandal and divorce, as the life of the Irish statesman Parnell and the experience of the well-known British Liberal Sir Charles Dilke show. In general, of course, only those were penalized who were so stupid as to let themselves be caught, but for them punishment could be unrelenting, especially if their vices were "unnatural" and their position conspicuous, as in Wilde's case.

Nevertheless, in spite of mealymouthed conventionality and rigid ideas about sexual morality, the last third of the nineteenth century showed a great increase in the publication of books, scientific and popular, fiction and nonfiction, whose purpose was to combat old-fashioned concepts of marriage, love, the social subordination of woman, prostitution, sexual education, problems of venereal disease and heredity, the protection of unmarried women, and homosexuality.

Three aspects of nineteenth-century culture operated to stimulate a concern with the sexual mores. First, the naturalistic movement in fiction—French and Russian even more than English—which described existing situations in forthright terms and revealed what sentimentality had long tried to conceal. Secondly, the rise of socialism stimulated many of its opponents to accept society's responsibility to do justice to the oppressed and exploited, not merely the poor, but also women, children, criminals, and others whom society either rejected entirely or treated as second-class citizens. Social rebels often objected to conventional marriage as oppressive to women and men alike, denying them freedom and genuine love. Thirdly, the emergence of Darwinism emphasized that man was a part of nature and that his sexuality had a natural right to expression.

One of the first cries of resisistance against the old morality, a bitter complaint against Victorian piety, especially where the family was concerned, was Samuel Butler's *The Way of all Flesh,* written in the 1870s but not published until 1903. It has been characterized by V.S. Pritchett as one of the time bombs of English literature. To think, as Pritchett remarks, that the book stayed for thirty years in Butler's desk in Clifford's Inn—ready to blow the Victorian family to pieces! Butler certainly was not a reformer; his novel merely pleaded for honesty. Its critical reception was veiled, but many of its readers found it a witty expression of what they long had felt and thought about fathers and mothers, about the power of money, and about the way in which marriage and the mores could entrap a young man. Nevertheless, Butler's novel was not primarily concerned with sexual liberty. Its focus was on the oppressive quality of British middle-class family life with its politely brutal subjection of the young and its continual emphasis on getting and having money.

At the end of the nineteenth century, the conflict between the old and new morality was further illustrated by the publication of a number of serious studies on human sexual life, outstanding among them are the works of Mantegazza, Forel, Havelock Ellis, and Bloch. The reception of their books was as sensational as their content. Bloch's *Das Sexualleben unserer Zeit* (*Contemporary Sexual Life*) sold sixty thousand copies in three years. Forel's *Die sexuelle Frage* (*The Sexual Problem*) was translated into sixteen languages. Although these books sold so surprisingly well, they also encountered much adverse criticism and resistance, including the equivalent of formal censorship. The first volume of Havelock Ellis's *Sex and Society* was confiscated when it appeared in England; the following volumes had to be printed and published in the United States. Interestingly enough, Ellis's book was defended by an organization in which George Bernard Shaw played an important role. Another interesting sidelight is given in an open letter by the court reporter Theodore Martin, which was sent to the press. Martin insisted that the law suppress Ellis's work, for according to Martin, the books would change society into a "collection of whores."

Yet these were the years of the cancan, the predecessor of the striptease, and of "art" photography that made glimpsed nudity even more suggestive by posing it against a black velvet background. The predecessor of today's bikini was praised by "Mad Nudists"; Isadora Duncan caused a scandal by dancing barefoot. The "good woman" did not know what sexual satisfaction was; and the "bad woman" knew *only* sexual satisfaction. No properly reared French girl would go out of her home alone, and even American girls with any pretensions to social standing required a chaperone when they went out with young men. When the Dutch Suffragettes organized an exposition called The Woman: 1813 to 1913, all the work for the exhibition in principle was done by women. Nevertheless, these very women thought that the good name of the enterprise would be hurt by the employment of female servants in the exposition restaurant. Why? Because in that time waitresses were expected to be sexually accessible and to earn their tips with the service of their bodies if required.

This was the time that the *Fliegende Blätter*, a German humor magazine, could publish a cartoon in which a little boy stares at a lady on a bicycle and exclaims, *"Aber Mutter, die Tante hat ja Beine"* ("But Mother, Auntie has legs").

But the turn of the century was also a time of doubt. The moral norms by which people had measured themselves began to be challenged more and more. The whole problem of sin is dealt with in Dostoevski's *Crime and Punishment*. Even English fiction could present a portrait of a "good" murderer, as Galsworthy did in *The First and the Last*. The whole subject of love was now beset by doubt rather than by the idea that sexual expression was sinful. The work of the Viennese doctor Arthur Schnitzler, for example, analyzes the intensity and the superficiality of love. *Reigen* and *Liebelei,* both plays by Schnitzler, present their bittersweet stories with a smile that is melancholy rather than mirthful.

About 1900 the number of divorces in Western Europe rose considerably; at the same time, discussion about divorce and free love came into full bloom. In 1906 Paris had a committee to reform marriage. Vienna had a similar committee. Bloch, the German sexologist, proposed a kind of trial marriage; the couple would remain together for five years, and if the marriage did not work out, then the parties could terminate without embarrassing—and expensive—formalities. Bloch thought to give his proposal the prestige of a classical literary background and cited Goethe's *Elective Affinities* in support of his plan (not very pointedly, one must say, since Goethe's novel deals with the unhappiness of a pair of married couples when the husband of one falls in love with the wife of the other but is far too conservative in social tone even to hint that unhappy marriages can properly be dissolved by anything but death).

While male novelists, dramatists, and students of society were considering problems of love and marriage from the point of view of men and society, women were dealing with those problems as they affected the emancipation of woman. That movement had begun, prosaically enough, when middle-class women, bored with inactivity and weary of continuous economic dependence, found respectable new ways of earning a living. Now the movement was growing more and more daring, demanding that women be allowed to vote, to express their own sexuality, and even to exist and function on a social and intellectual level as independent beings rather than as appendages of an established male reputation.

Lou Andreas-Salomé, one of Freud's outstanding pupils and the lover of Rilke and Nietzsche, attempted to analyze both women and men; she refused to restrict herself as a writer to the expected subject of woman. In doing so, she rejected the traditional psychological and social dogma of the passive woman. Of course, sharp reactions and rejections to the emancipated woman occurred, notably by the psychologist P. G. Mobius and a young Viennese philosopher Otto Weininger, as well as, of course, Strindberg and Nietzsche. None of these men could accept the emancipation of women, the right of woman to her essential human right of equal treatment, equal opportunity, equal responsibility. They saw emancipation rather as a total rejection of the female role. Weininger in *Geschlecht und Charakter* (*Sex and Character*) maintains that the intelligence of active, gifted women is only the result of their identification with men. Strindberg's obvious and inherent hatred of women stems from his personal insecurity, which led him to fear women.

But the struggle had only begun. Shame still prevailed. Sexuality was shameful in itself; deviations of sexual behavior were even more shameful. Guy de Maupassant, who wrote so movingly about lesbian love in *La femme de Paul,* and Marcel Proust, who explored homosexuality so thoroughly in *A la recherche du temps perdu,* tried to free themselves from the bondage of their shame about their sexuality, but one may wonder whether they achieved that goal. The full liberation of sexuality, which entailed a rejection of all the notions about sexuality that had prevailed during the nineteenth century, was a long way off—if indeed it has arrived at all. Certainly the liberation of sexuality was not accomplished by anything discussed in this chapter. For much of the liberation occurred among cultivated people, often among rebellious intellectuals. Doubt about conventional sex morality—and particularly free expression of such doubt—had not seeped down to the middle and lower classes. Sexual prejudices, like all prejudices, are hard to fight and overcome. The writers, scientific philosophers, philosophic investigators, and observers of culture and society who have been discussed here were far ahead of their time. The future might accept their viewpoint; in their own day, they were censored, censured, and accused of promoting immorality.

Imperial Germany may be labeled the great political success story of nineteenth-century Europe. Out of a loose confederation of rather poor states, energetic bureaucrats and military leaders, with Otto von Bismarck as their final guide (there had been other successful Prussian premiers), had used organization, diplomacy, and war to create a unified nation, which, after 1870, became a formidable world power. Prosperous, culturally active, and curiously vulgar, Wilhelmine Germany—the empire Wilhelm II took over when he pushed the Iron Chancellor out of power in 1890—became almost as notorious for sexual misbehavior in high places as it was noteworthy for technological progress and scientific achievement.

The cultural tone of Imperial Germany was set by the Kaiser and his Empress: Both delighted in the pompous and the gaudy; both abhorred modernity. The Emperor was renowned for bombastic speeches; the Empress, for her inclination to meddle. In the opera, for example, she tinkered with the staging of Strauss's *Salome;* she forbade *Rosenkavalier* to open in Berlin. Wilhelm dismissed Hugo von Tschudi, director of the Berlin National Gallery, because of Tschudi's subversively modern taste in art. Wilhelm's law courts prosecuted Käthe Kollwitz for her proletarian posters. The new literature turned the stomachs of the governing classes: when Bavarian statesman Prince Chlodwig zu Hohenlohe-Schillingfurst went to see *Hanneles Himmelfahrt* in 1893, he had

THE GERMAN
SEXOLOGISTS AND
THEIR EMPIRE

to wash away the taste of that dramatic monstrosity with a good dose of caviar and champagne.[1]

Philistine and oppressive though Wilhelmine Germany might be, it was not a dictatorship. In spite of imperial and noble hostility, the modern movement in art and literature continued. It produced Expressionism, nonobjective painting, the political songs of Walter Mehring, the prose of Heinrich Mann, the eccentric drama of Franz Wedekind, and Carl Sternheim's bitter portrait of the heroic life of the bourgeoisie: vulgar display, crass scramble for status, and hypocritical pretention to morality and national honor. "After us, collapse!" exclaims one of Sternheim's characters in a play written during the last year of peace. "We are ripe."

Where France, at the turn of the twentieth century, was racked by political dissension generated by the Dreyfus case, Wilhelmine Germany was afflicted—and titillated—by tales of lurid misconduct in high places and particularly by sensational revelations of homosexuality among men influential in public life. "Unnatural vice" was probably no more prevalent during these decades than it had been, nor was it any more evident in Germany than elsewhere in Europe. German law bore as severely on homosexuals as law did anywhere: Paragraph 175 of the Penal Code punished sex relations between men (similar conduct between women was not legally actionable; apparently female sex deviation was not of sufficient concern to the state to warrant the law's intervention). The code was selectively enforced, to be sure, generally bearing hardest on the poor and insignificant, but it was the law.

Nevertheless, by the turn of the century German homosexuals were becoming more and more conspicuous. Foreigners pointed accusing fingers. The French called homosexuality the German vice, as they called sadomasochism, and particularly flagellation, the darling vice of the English. (Sexual aberrations and venereal disease are, almost universally, said to be of foreign origin.) More and more rumors were heard charging that sexual deviates held high posts in the German army, the civil service, and the diplomatic corps.

Should deviates be dismissed, it was asked, even if their work was satisfactory? Many influential people thought not. To prosecute homosexuals for violating the penal code or to discharge them from their jobs seemed an unwarrantable intrusion into private life. Imperial Germany might not be a stronghold of political or civil liberty, but at least, liberal opinion held, it dealt with sexual deviation more generously—and more realistically—than such countries as England, which boasted of their allegiance to freedom.

But liberal opinion began to shift in 1910, for political reasons, one suspects, rather than for reasons associated with a revival of stringent sexual morality. In 1910 *Die Zukunft,* a respected Berlin magazine, declared that a clique of homosexuals at the Imperial Court were cutting the Emperor off from his proper, responsible advisers. The homosexual *camarilla* (one might say *kitchen cabinet* if emperors ever entered kitchens) was leading the Kaiser into making dangerous decisions or, worse still, encouraging him in indecision.

Historians of the period have not yet explained how the Emperor came to be so strongly influenced by homosexual courtiers; certainly there was no doubt that Wilhelm II was completely heterosexual in behavior.[2] Yet a group of *Urnings**—a favored euphemism of the time— had indeed secured the Emperor's confidence. They hedged him about, excluded him from any but formal contact with his ministers and other possible advisers, and so constituted themselves into a secret, irresponsible, although not entirely invisible, government. For it was evident to many observers that the Emperor listened to the camarilla more readily than he heard the views of his own official ministers of state.

Thus homosexuals and their habits became a political issue. Few

---

* The word *Urnings* was coined by Karl Heinrich Ulrichs (1825–1895), who was a high-placed official in the German government. He wrote several essays on homosexuality, mostly a defense of homosexuality. All were published in Latin. He also wrote some homosexual poetry, which was published in German under the title *Auf Bienchens Flügeln* (Leipzig, 1875).

Germans, even those most conservative and obedient to authority, were willing to be governed by a court clique of perverts. Since the Kaiser was supposed to be unaware of the true character of the men to whom he had given his confidence, the man who would open the Kaiser's eyes and break the power of this dangerous breed would be performing a patriotic service. Maximilian Harden, publisher of *Die Zukunft,* undertook this task with remarkable courage, since those he attacked were of distinguished family as well as important position, and social deference was a strong force in Germany.

Harden accepted the risk of attacking those who would be called his "betters" for a higher purpose than that of giving his readers spicy gossip about the glamorous figures who occupied high places. More was involved than the conduct of a little group of immoral men. A vast conspiracy existed, Harden maintained, involving people far distant from the German Court and its intrigues. Urnings everywhere, in Germany and outside, constituted an international fraternity. These catamites (an abusive term for homosexuals, which had unpleasant overtones of passivity) were linked in a dubious comradeship far stronger than that represented by monastic orders, Jesuits, or Freemasons (three other bogeymen cherished by those who accepted conspiracy theories of history). The ties among Urnings bound men of all classes, creeds, parties, and nations into both a league for mutual defense and an aggressive movement to acquire power.

Urnings were everywhere, at Court, in army and navy commands, at the editorial desks of newspapers, at tradesmen's counters and teachers' blackboards, even on the Bench. All were ready to protect one another, Harden argued. Many scorned normal men as insufficiently differentiated beings, capable of only crude pleasures and commonplace loyalties. Because homosexuals constituted an international brotherhood, they were linked in a chain of betrayal. Their loyalty to one another outweighed their loyalty to the state. Even when Urnings wanted to be faithful Germans, their involvement in acts forbidden by law and their desire to keep their habits secret from relatives and employers made

them easy victims of blackmailers, who could force them into revealing military secrets or yielding to political cabals. (Heterosexual lapses might also subject offenders to blackmail, but since such lapses were mere human weakness rather than "unnatural sin," revelation would cause less public harm.[3])

Similar arguments had been heard two centuries earlier when homosexual courtiers of Louis XIV had founded a mutual aid association of their own at Versailles. Harden could point to similar projects in Germany. In 1901 Count Günther von der Schulenburg had sent a circular letter to a number of high-ranking homosexuals. The circular began: "I beg you to permit a person of equal rank and similar tastes to express his ideas about a union of noble Urnings." This curious project had a primarily social purpose, but the count also proposed that the league operate as a brotherhood of titled homosexuals united to protect themselves against intrusive legal inquiry. In order to create the brotherhood, prospective members were asked to pay a modest annual fee. For, said the count, "without support from noble-minded *Urnings,* I can do nothing."

Certainly this kind of organization sounds more farcical—and pathetic—than threatening to the state. But, according to Harden, Schulenburg was only a secondary character in the ugly drama being played at the Imperial Court. The "stars" must be exposed and punished in order that the Emperor and the people might be properly protected. Chief among the men Harden feared was Prince Philip zu Eulenburg und Hertefeld, a member of the Prussian House of Lords, formerly the Prussian Minister in Bavaria and the German Ambassador in Vienna. Although the Prince no longer held any public office, he was completely at home in Court circles. He accompanied the Emperor on all his long journeys, had ready access to him, and enjoyed his complete confidence. It was this intimate of the Emperor who was the real object of Harden's revelations.

The publisher had first learned about Eulenburg's tastes from Bismarck, immediately after his dismissal from the post of Chancellor.

Because Bismarck's statements had been too general to impress a public that demanded factual evidence, a number of years went by before Harden was able to use the information. Harden was able to act only after the Kaiser removed another important statesman, Privy Councillor von Holstein, for decades the "gray eminence" of the Foreign Office. Von Holstein in his anger gave Harden more concrete information than Bismarck had thought it discreet to provide.[4]

Harden had his facts, but printing them in his journal was a risky enterprise: highly placed homosexuals do not habitually indulge themselves in public view. It seemed certain that Prince Eulenburg had abnormal habits, but it was hard to prove him to be a practicing homosexual—and only evidence of that would bring him within reach of the law.

Harden opened his campaign cautiously. His first articles on the Court camarilla in *Die Zukunft* (1906) were so obscure in their allusions that the uninitiated reader scarcely knew what was being talked about. Insiders, however, would soon be able to interpret the allusions and to take malicious pleasure in their understanding. Harden's targets, and the Emperor, could easily draw the obvious conclusions. But the Court did not move. Then Harden grew more daring and named names. The Prince brought suit.

The situation now began to resemble the Oscar Wilde case, but the proceedings had a different outcome. Eulenburg denied all the charges on oath. The judges decided that Harden's evidence was insufficient to prove his statements accurate. Accordingly, a Berlin court sentenced Harden to four months' imprisonment for libel.

His conviction did not close the affair, however. Attacks on Harden by another newspaper allowed the publisher to reopen the case, this time before a magistrate's court in Munich. Now luck swung in Harden's direction. After the Berlin trial, a milkman from Upper Bavaria had come to Harden's counsel and blurted: "He [Eulenburg] made camarilla with me."

The illiterate milkman's belief that "camarilla" had sexual reference

THE GERMAN SEXOLOGISTS
AND THEIR EMPIRE

gave Harden his key to vindication. This witness could safely speak the truth, for he could no longer be punished—his "camarilla" doings had all taken place far too long ago when he was a boy of nineteen working on a boat on the Starnberger See. A "fine gentleman"—who was the Prince himself—had made overtures to him and had finally had his way. Eulenburg had been generous; he invited the young sailor to his castle, treated him sumptuously, and gave him a present of 1500 marks, more than the youth's wages for a year.

Soon the milkman's testimony was bolstered by a report of similar experiences by a Starnberger See fisherman. The new witnesses could not be shaken. Evidently Eulenburg had lied under oath. Legal proceedings were brought, but the Prince was too sick to face trial. Politically, this signified nothing; the Prince had to leave Court circles, for he stood condemned in the eyes of public opinion. Other cases were also brought; the most noteworthy was against Count Kuno von Moltke, governor of Berlin and adjutant to the Emperor. Those proceedings were inconclusive, but the very fact of their being brought was significant.

Harden achieved his purpose; the camarilla vanished from the Imperial Court. Whether Wilhelm II was better advised after dismissing the Urnings from his entourage is not our concern here. Certainly, proceedings like the Eulenburg and the von Moltke affairs continued to hold public interest for years. The trials did much to discredit both the monarchy and the nobility. People who had been entirely unaware of homosexuality as anything but a disturbing whisper or an unseemly joke now devoured details about the unseemly and even sordid behavior of men in high places. Those who should be establishing standards of conduct were breaking the law. If leaders among the aristocracy were this "tainted," who, asked the unsophisticated, could be trusted? It became common to wonder whether friends and neighbors had rendered themselves subject to punishment under Paragraph 175 of the Penal Code. And beyond the political and sociological significance of the trials was the evidence of the popular reaction to them: Prejudice in respect to sex-

ual morality made Wilhelm's Germans and King Edward's Englishmen brothers under the skin.

Yet, so far as educated Germans were concerned, they had had reasonably good opportunity to learn about the full range of sexual behavior. For nineteenth-century Germany and Austria produced an impressive array of learned students of sexuality. These men were pioneers, the first to deal with sexuality as a physiological and psychological discipline in its own right. Why these pioneers should have been German, it is hard to say. Certainly, German culture was as characterized by a rigidity of standards and an emphasis on discipline in the area of sexual behavior as elsewhere. The German family structure was thoroughly authoritarian and patriarchal. The double standard of morals prevailed here as elsewhere: The purity of good women was protected by the accessibility of prostitutes, and lapses from marital fidelity entailed social punishment for women in a far more severe degree than it did for men.

Perhaps this situation helps to explain the emergence of German sexology. Rigidity and repression created curiosity. Those who could, did, as it were; and those whose inhibitions or personal problems prevented doing, studied. As a result, the scientific study of sexual behavior made its first appearnce in German-speaking countries.

The foregoing conjectures may do some injustice to such noteworthy scholars as Magnus Hirschfeld, Richard Krafft-Ebing, Albert Moll, Isidor Sadger, Albert Eulenburg (who is, of course, not to be confused with Prince Philip), Ivan Bloch, André Forel, and to a certain degree, Wilhelm Stekel. The study of sexuality was a new and rather scandalous field of inquiry when these men began their work. What, after all, did nineteenth-century people know about sex—on other than the practical level. It is necessary to reemphasize that, although more enlightened attitudes were emerging, the effects of repressiveness were marked. Responsible discussion of sexuality was extremely difficult. After all, sex was taboo, something one could not and should not discuss.[5] Medical men themselves were often blatantly ignorant about both sexual phenomena and sexual pathology. Even psychiatrists knew little about the field.

There was, of course, much information about venereal disease and some knowledge about aberrations of sexual behavior. For these manifestations frequently were encountered by physicians. Consequently, the abnormal aspects of sexuality had received more studious attention than behavior that was regarded as normal. After all, psychiatrists and physicians generally encountered people's sex lives only when a patient presented specific symptoms for treatment or, less often, confided some unhappiness or anxiety. So doctors knew about homosexuality. Some knew about sadomasochism; others, perhaps, had some awareness of fetishism. To only a few doctors, might a patient say ''I am a transvestite'' and expect a reaction other than one of distaste or shocked horror. With this kind of ignorance so common among those presumed to be professionally competent, small wonder that little about any of these sexual deviations was known to the average educated man. And he was even more ignorant, perhaps, about what he considered to be normal sexual behavior.

Nevertheless, for the layman, discussion of sex continued to offer a kind of appeal to prurience that even serious studies expensively presented could not discourage. And physicians, particularly alienists (we call them psychiatrists nowadays), continued to publish case material. Indeed, a psychiatrist could do little more for a patient who came to him with a problem arising from sexual deviation than to listen and record. Most psychiatrists were themselves still burdened with guilt and repression where sexuality was concerned. Further, they lacked information. Little was known about the dynamics of sexuality, and small effort was made to learn. What then could even a Krafft-Ebing or a Magnus Hirschfeld do to help a harried sadist or a compulsive yet morally troubled homosexual? Urge him to consult his clergyman? Counsel the exertion of willpower and prescribe sedatives, cold baths, and conventional behavior?

Yet, though nineteenth-century psychiatrists could offer little help other than sympathetic moralizing, they could describe aberrant behavior. And many a sexual deviant may have drawn some psychological relief from knowing that he was not unique. The German (and Austrian) students of sexuality who created a new discipline during the nineteenth century did much to free discussion of sexuality from Victorian restrictions. Such liberalization was a by-product, of course, rather than an intended result. Except for Hirschfeld and perhaps Ivan Bloch, few of the German sexologists would have been either aware or approving of the effect of their work; the liberalization of sexual expression, whether in word or action, was not their purpose.

Very little of the foregoing applies to Magnus Hirschfeld (1868–1935). He completed his medical studies in 1894 and soon became interested in the problems of sexuality and the relation between those problems and prevalent trauma and taboos. In the early years of the twentieth century, Hirschfeld founded the Institute of Sexual Science in Berlin and continued active through the first decades of the twentieth century. The institute, under his leadership, sought to develop an understanding of sexuality in terms of the problems people confronted in dealing with their sexual lives. He and his associates prepared a number of important studies, two of which have recently been reissued. One deals with sexual behavior during World War I, the other with the years between the end of the war and the beginning of the Hitler regime. These books are landmarks in the history of sexology and provide a mine of information about the effect of war and social disruption on the sexual behavior of soldiers and civilians, the impoverished, and their exploiters. [6]

Some of Hirschfeld's humane concern with sexual problems may be attributed to his own experience. Homosexual himself, [7] he had a peculiarly intimate awareness of the kind of burden that society placed upon the sexual deviant. His own scientific interests may well have grown out of an effort to understand himself. Hirschfeld is best known for *Die Homosexualität des Mannes und des Weibes,* [8] an outstanding study of homosexuality. His *Geschlechtskunde* presented the first comprehensive statement on human sexuality.[9] His studies on the sexual life of adults both in *Das erotische Weltbild* (1929) and *Geschlechtsleben der Erwachsenen* (1913) stand as landmarks in sexology. Undoubtedly, he and his associates would have published further studies; the archives of the institute were crammed with valuable research material. Unfortunately much of this was lost in the 1930s when Hitler came to power, and Hirschfeld's books and his bust were publicly burned. Fortunately, Hirschfeld left Germany in 1930 on a world tour and never returned. He gave 176 lectures all over the world and was honored by many professional societies, including the Academy of Medicine in New York, where he was introduced by Dr. A. A. Brill, an outstanding pupil of Freud's. Brill later contributed an introduction to Hirschfeld's *Curious Sex Customs in the Far East,*[10] which was one result of his travels.[11]

Noteworthy is Hirschfeld's attitude toward the possibility of medical management of sexual problems as people encounter them in their daily lives. He does not offer much resembling what might today be considered psychotherapy, although he was more interested than were many of his fellow workers in the field of sexology in such an approach to distortions of sexual behavior. Indeed, he became a member in good standing of the Berlin Psychoanalytic Society.[12]

Hirschfeld's work is interesting, but it does not approach the pioneering significance of that of Richard Krafft-Ebing (1840–1902), who is the acknowledged father of the systematic study of sexuality. His major work, *Psychopathia Sexualis,* appeared in 1886 and still holds its position in the study of varieties of sexual behavior.[13] Krafft-Ebing paints a picture based on numerous case studies, but he was not much interested in the dynamics of pathological behavior nor in therapeutic work with sexual deviants. His followers, Ivan Bloch and André Forel, particularly, took a less restricted view. They were interested in the sexual aspects of ethnology, folklore, education, the administration of criminal law, the possibility of eugenics, and the relationship between the study of sexuality and the history of philosophy, ethics in particular, of literature and of culture in general. Bloch (1872–1922) was especially interested in the history of sexual customs [14] and certain aspects of sexuality. [15] In a period when abnormal human behavior was still described with few references to sexuality, Bloch discussed a wide spectrum of sexual custom and conduct.

André Forel's main interest lay in the field of sexual ethics, the social aspect of sexuality. *Die Sexuelle Frage* was among the earliest works to present a forthright discussion of the sexual side of marriage. Forel went further than the marriage-manual approach, however, for he was concerned with the need to transform the institution of marriage and make it more relevant to the world of the late nineteenth and early twentieth centuries. Although Forel lacked a grasp of the dynamics of sexual development, his conclusions as well as his material disturbed many of his more conventional contemporaries. Later research has outmoded many of his reports, but modern workers in the field continue to acknowledge their debt to Forel.

Albert Moll, Albert Eulenburg, and Isidor Sadger are not as well known as Bloch, Forel, Hirschfeld, and Krafft-Ebing, yet their work on sexuality and sexual pathology has much to offer readers who command a reading knowledge of German; neither Moll's *Libido Sexualis* [16] nor Sadger's *Sexuelle Neuropathie* has yet been translated.

Of all these German pioneers in sexology, Magnus Hirschfeld was the only one to become well known to the lay public. He coined the label ''the third sex'' to express all forms and nuances of homosexual behavior, including the sexual intermediate stages. Hirschfeld went on to take the (in his time) unusual position of urging that members of the third sex be protected by law rather than prosecuted as criminals and made to feel outlaws from society. The policy Hirschfeld recommended was not anywhere adopted in the western world. Rather, his reputation for ferreting out and revealing forbidden varieties of sexuality was strengthened by his frequent court appearances as an expert witness. The Munich humorous weekly *Simplizissimus* caricatured this phase of Hirschfeld's work in a cartoon sketch of the Weimar Poets Monument where Goethe and Schiller stand hand in hand. Goethe is shown withdrawing his hand and saying: "Fritz, let go, here comes Hirschfeld!"

This caricaturist's attitude, with its emphasis on debunking, is reflected on a more serious plane in the emergence of a new form of biography, *pathography*, which discussed political and artistic leaders in terms of their sexual life. Isidor Sadger wrote a noteworthy study of the poet Heinrich von Kleist, which tried to show how Kleist's homosexuality affected his treatment of plot and character. Dr. Gaston Vorberg, who practiced in Munich, was much interested in the lives of intellectuals and wrote pathographies of a number of artists and philosophers, including Nietzsche, the poet Nikolaus Lenau, and the composer Hugo Wolf. Gaston Vorberg also produced studies on Vincent van Gogh (probably one of the first to appear) and Jean Jacques Rousseau, Lord Byron, and the German playwright Karl Stauffer.

Psychoanalysts, of course, as that discipline developed, contributed not only to sexology proper but also to the literature of pathography. Noteworthy contributions in this field are Arthur Kielholz's studies of the German mystic Jacob Böhme and Eduard Hitschmann's work on the Swiss poet Gottfried Keller. One might put Freud's essay on Leonardo into this category as one could also put Wilhelm Stekel's studies of impotence, frigidity, fetishism, and sadism into the category of sexology. But Freud and Stekel are more appropriately discussed elsewhere.[17]

Interestingly, it was Austrian poets, novelists, psychologists, and critics of society who, especially before World War I, transmitted to German audiences their own concern with decadence and their own efforts to come to terms with Eros and sexuality. Freud, Hugo von Hofmannsthal, and Arthur Schnitzler had as many, or perhaps more, readers in Berlin, Munich, and Frankfurt as they had in Vienna. Schnitzler was popular outside the German-speaking countries; von Hofmannsthal was well known both as a poet and as Richard Strauss's librettist, and Freud's influence was worldwide.[18]

The liberation of sexuality is a problem that continues to concern students of society, psychologists, psychotherapists, and ordinary men and women in trying to lead fruitful and satisfactory lives. Insofar as such liberation has been achieved or, more accurately, insofar as more people envision the possibility of achieving such a liberation, our debt to the nineteenth-century German sexologists is considerable. They brought forbidden subjects into the open field of scientific discussion and so, ultimately, furthered the weakening of sexual taboos and the increase of sexual enlightenment.

Sexuality in nineteenth-century England has chroniclers aplenty, but they preferred either to write fiction or to use assumed names.[1] To be sure, many intellectuals did express their sexuality freely, but these men tended to cluster together in groups, like that which centered about Wilde or, on another level, the writers and artists who made Bloomsbury famous. One might also mention the free-floating pornography, which apparently found a ready market in Victorian England.[2]

Yet the era is still named for that formidable Queen, who dominated the English moral scene for the better part of the nineteenth century. Queen Victoria set the moral tone not only for her own citizens, but also for the numerous relatives who populated royal and ducal courts all over the Continent. Certainly, no woman had a more exalted notion of the deference that was her due. An example of what the Queen thought her position to be is given by Elisabeth Longford in *Victoria R.I.*, in which she describes a project for a match between Prince Alfred of England and the Grand Duchess Marie, the only daughter of Emperor Alexander II of Russia. Victoria wished to inspect the bride on British soil. The Emperor felt otherwise and called Victoria "a silly fool." To smooth matters, the Empress, backed by Victoria's daughter Princess Alice of Hesse, suggested that the Queen come to Germany and view the bride there. The ruler of Great Britain exploded: "You have *entirely*

3 | THE LONELY
ENGLISHMAN:
HAVELOCK ELLIS

taken the Russian side, and I do *not* think, dear Child, that *you* should tell me who have been nearly *twenty years* longer on the throne than the Emperor of Russia and am the Doyenne of Sovereigns and who am a reigning sovereign which the Empress is not, *what I ought to do. I think I know that.* The proposal received on *Wednesday* for me to be at *Cologne* . . . tomorrow, was one of the *coolest* things I ever heard. . . ." [3]

On the question of the morality of Queen Victoria and her influence in the nineteenth century it is interesting to note that certain episodes may be interpreted to show that Queen Victoria may have been less than a model of Victorian behavior. After all, her lasting attachment to John Brown, the head of her stables, was scarcely in accord with the prevailing ideals of either social or moral conduct. [4] Replacing a husband, and Prince Consort, with a groom was scarcely consonant with what Englishmen expected of their widowed Queen. In *Leisure and Pleasure in the Nineteenth Century,* Stella Margetson writes that it was not the Queen but Prince Albert who really set England an example. According to the Duke of Wellington, Prince Albert was "extremely straitlaced . . . whereas she [the young Queen] was rather the other way." The Prince was shocked by Victoria's headstrong behavior and by her passion for dancing and playing games. In spite of earnest advice from his uncle, King Leopold of Belgium, and his tutor, Baron Stockmar, Albert was not at all happy at first as the bridegroom of the Queen. "The difficulty of filling my place with proper dignity is that I am only the husband and not the master of the house," he wrote his friend Prince Lowenstein. It irked Albert extremely to have Victoria dismiss him from the room when her ministers came to see her, refusing to discuss with him even the most minor affairs of state. [5]

The dark obverse of nineteenth-century English social and sexual life has lately received much attention. Steven Marcus, in *The Other Victorians,* has rescued from obscurity the work of sexologist William Acton (1814–1875), of Henry Spencer Ashbee (1834–1900), the bibliographer of pornography, and of the anonymous author of *My Secret Life.*

Marcus has woven these works into a connected theory of nineteenth-century sexual ideology (in the Marxian sense of false consciousness). In particular, Marcus has drawn attention to the central role played in Victorian thinking about sex, as expounded by Samuel Smiles in *Thrift* (1875): that the expenditure, or loss, of semen is equated with expenditure, or loss, of money.

This mechanical identification, neatly summed up in the then current vulgarism of "spend" for "ejaculate," provides a valuable key to the hostility toward sex that dominated practically the whole century.[6] Extravagant young men "sowed their wild oats," with the help of the army of girls driven on the street by starvation wages—or thriftier, they soothed themselves by masturbating. And they reaped, it was claimed, a harvest of insanity, debility, and disease. Their more cautious contemporaries did their utmost to conserve money and seed alike. And when, in spite of cold baths, prayer, and other exercises, nature wetted their dreams and their bed linen, they hastened to quack doctors, preferring the physical agonies of cautery and catheter to the mental agonies of guilt and fear.

Those who doubt that the money-semen theory prevailed in middle-class minds a hundred years ago should ponder the case of Holmes Coote (1817–1872), a surgeon at St. Bartholomew's Hospital and an expert on diseases of the tongue and joints. He told a meeting of medical men in 1866: "Among the young there was no cause of insanity more common than indulging in habits that he would not further particularize, but which were known to result in a most complete bodily and mental prostration."[7] This learned partisan of the masturbation-drive-you-mad school died of general paralysis *"with delusions of boundless wealth."* [8]

Yet one should not think that English sexuality under Victoria was limited to marriage, masturbation, or chastity. Prostitution and all other forms of sexual entertainment were widespread under her reign. As widespread, although perhaps harder to come by since prostitution was tolerated whereas pornography might be prosecuted, was the peculiar

English taste for erotica, often pretending to be "translated" from the French. It must be admitted, however, that defense to Mrs. Grundy did not improve the quality of this sub-literature. It is an illusion, spread by those who seek to get us back to an age of censorship, that pornography becomes specially "perverted" in a period of literary and sexual freedom. On the contrary, in periods of literary and sexual repression—when reputable publishers are jailed, as, for example, Henry Vizetelly was in 1889 for issuing works of literary merit—when society cannot acknowledge the reality of the sexual impulse and is therefore riddled with hypocrisy that writing about sex becomes clandestine and obsessed with the infliction of pain and the corruption of the immature. To banish erotic realism from literature is to damage both. Peter Fryer remarks, "In the course of the nineteenth century, pornography becomes steadily less concerned with copulation and more with cruelty." [9]

The Victorian era, then, cherished an ideal of sexual propriety but was often more prurient than pure in its behavior. Pornography might flourish in such an atmosphere, but scientific research was more difficult. Nevertheless, nineteenth-century England did produce a few sexologists. Two of them, Havelock Ellis and Edward Carpenter, were men of great intellectual and literary gifts. Both men led rather stormy lives. Edward Carpenter was a homosexual who did not keep his sexual preference a secret, an amazingly daring position in a country where the law punished homosexual behavior (when it actually was punished). Ellis, for the major part of his life, was married to a lesbian, Edith Lees, whom he passionately loved in spite of obvious limitations on their sexual relationship. [10] One may wonder why Ellis tangled himself in such a marriage, for the answer Ellis himself gives in his autobiography seems far from sufficient. [11] But no adequate explanation seems possible, for all his willingness to talk of himself, and for all the exploration of writers who have dealt with his life, Havelock Ellis emerges as an essentially lonely man, who sheltered his privacy behind a cloud of words.

Ellis's work does not cover sexuality alone, but deals with anthropol-

THE LONELY ENGLISHMAN:
HAVELOCK ELLIS

ogy, sociology, psychology, travel, art, religion, literary criticism, translation, including fiction, and even some very worthwhile columns in the daily press. His erudition was amazing. At an early age he inaugurated the famous Mermaid Series of unexpurgated reprints of Elizabethan and Restoration dramatists; he edited the volumes himself, wrote some of the introductions, and persuaded Swinburne to write a general introduction to the series. Then Ellis conceived the idea of a series of books on contemporary science. He edited each volume and translated some of them himself, and with exceptional skill. Although the advance of knowledge has made much of the material obsolete, the project itself was a monumental achievement. In *Affirmations,* a volume of literary essays, Ellis helped introduce Huysmans and Ibsen to English readers. His book *The Soul of Spain* is a gem, as is his Australian idyll *Kangacreek.* Ellis's intimate journals, *Impressions and Comments,* give further insight into the mind and life of this English genius. Ellis did his most noteworthy work in the field of sexology in the *Studies of the Psychology of Sex.* This large work can still be described as "an encyclopedia of sexual behavior unmatched in the world," which drew upon literary sources quite unknown to Freud. Furthermore, with the *Studies* and in other books as well, Ellis helped to break open "the conspiracy of silence about sex, a tremendous feat under the formidable gaze of Her Imperial Majesty Queen Victoria." [12]

Ellis concentrated on describing sexual behavior rather than explaining it. He developed no substantial hypotheses to account for the variations of sexual expression. Inevitably one wonders about the relationship of his work to Freud's and, particularly, about Freud's attitude toward Ellis's research. On the whole, Freud appears cool. When Ellis sent him the final volume of *Studies* in 1928, Freud replied with rather chilly politeness, noting that he himself continued working out of necessity but without creative exuberance. Almost, one feels, Freud is rebuking his correspondent's intellectual fertility, his undiminished propensity for publishing and filling people's bookshelves. [13] Elsewhere, Freud was even less complimentary. In conversation with the psychiatrist

Joseph Wortis, Freud said: "He [Ellis] speaks freely of things about which he has no knowledge at all without so much as concerning himself with the literature." [14]

Ellis himself acknowledged that *Studies in the Psychology of Sex* was not a systematic work. As he wrote in his autobiography, "It was, as my nature is, a natural growth. . . . When I see myself praised, as sometimes happens, for my erudition, I smile, for I am not a scholar who lives surrounded by books but a dreamer lying in the sunshine, and erudition is the smallest qualification for work that I have done. The supreme qualification has doubtless been a deep inner sympathy and an ever closer personal touch with other human beings, combined with an artist's power of expression. It was thus that during long years I acquired a vast amount of miscellaneous material to be woven into my *Studies,* and incidentally acquired the undeserved reputation of immense encyclopedic erudition, whereas it is the artistic skill and critical judgment expended in using the material rather than its mere accumulation for which credit should be assigned, if credit is due." [15]

The first volume appeared in Germany, incidentally, in 1896; when it was published in English in 1897, it was immediately suppressed. The sixth volume was published in Germany in 1910; it was not published in England until 1935. *Studies in the Psychology of Sex* is not only Ellis's most important work but also Edwardian England's principal contribution to psychological knowledge.[16] *Studies* is primarily a work of synthesis, derived from a vast range of scientific and literary sources rather than from primary research, but the value of the book is not reduced by this fact. For what Ellis did in his synthesis was to document a new attitude toward sex, which is essentially the attitude prevalent in the twentieth century.

Ellis took sexuality as a category of human behavior, which expressed itself in manifold ways and is available for study from many points of view—biological, sociological, historical, and anthropological. His approach is not pathological, that is, he is not concerned only with the abnormal in sexual behavior but with all sexual behavior.

Ellis was the first English writer to treat homosexuality as a natural form of human behavior rather than an "unnatural vice." He was also the first to study autoeroticism (a term he coined), and to describe the evolution of modesty.

Above all, Havelock Ellis was the first English writer on sex to be at once objective and readable. Before Ellis, writers on sex had either elaborately avoided details or had followed Krafft-Ebing's practice: "In order that unqualified persons should not become readers," he wrote in the preface to *Psychopathia Sexualis,* "the author saw himself compelled to choose a title understood only by the learned, and also, where possible, to express himself in *terminis technicis.* It seemed necessary to give certain particularly revolting portions in Latin." [17] Ellis, on the contrary, assumed that sex was a subject in which all adults were qualified to take an interest, and he wrote for the general reader. His contribution to sexology is best understood if one sees him not as scientist or psychologist but as a "philosopher" of sex. He made a beginning in the long task of persuading Englishmen that sexual behavior was not only a matter of conventional morality but also of human instinct. And he gave circulation to two important but unpopular ideas: that sexual deviants were not all vicious and that judgments about sexual behavior should be based on natural and humane considerations rather than on social and even legal conventions. Havelock Ellis's own judgment of his achievement in *Studies* is a just one: "I had done mankind a service which mankind needed, and which, it seemed, I alone was fitted to do. I had helped to make the world, and to make the world in the only way it can be made, the interior way, by liberating the human spirit." [18]

The work of Havelock Ellis has been severely criticized as unscientific. Because he derived his information from existing knowledge rather than from personally obtained primary sources, he was an amateur in the eyes of scientific sociologists and psychologists. But again, Ellis's contribution, especially in his own Victorian and Edwardian age, was to liberate sex from ignorance and repression and to free man's natural impulses once more.

One of Ellis's most important contributions to the study of sexuality was the first volume of *Studies,* which was seized and destroyed by the police. This, of course, was not unusual in the last decades of the nineteenth century. Nor was it limited to English writers. The works of Ivan Bloch were also destroyed and suppressed by the police. The common justification for such suppression was that such books might fall into the hands of the young and ignorant: scientific information about sex, it was assumed, would inflame and corrupt young minds. Consider, as an example, the reasons given by *The Lancet,* a well-known English medical journal, for its failure to take adequate notice of *Sexual Inversion:*
"When Mr. Havelock Ellis' book was sent to us for review we did not review it, and our reason for this neglect of the work of the editor of the 'Contemporary Science Series' was . . . its method of publication. Why was it not published through a house able to take proper measures for introducing it as a scientific book to a scientific audience? . . . We believe that the book would fall into the hands of readers totally unable to derive benefit from it as a work of science and very ready to draw evil lessons from its necessarily disgusting passages. It must be pointed out, too, that a more than ordinary danger is attached to Mr. Havelock Ellis' work as a book for laymen in that the author's views happen to be that sexual inversion is far more prevalent than we believe it to be and that the legislature does injustice to many by regarding as crimes the practices with which it is bound up. He has failed to convince us on these points; and his historical references and the 'human documents' with which he has been furnished will, we think, fail equally to convince medical men that homosexuality is anything else than acquired and a depraved manifestation of the sexual passion: but, be that as it may, it is especially important that such matters should not be discussed by the men of the street." [19]

This *Lancet* statement shows how narrow and restrictive even the medical profession was in nineteenth-century England. Sexuality was a "dirty secret," and it ought to be kept so. Medical men might discuss sexual pathology with each other—behind the shield of Latinate

THE LONELY ENGLISHMAN:
HAVELOCK ELLIS

terms, but the less the man (or boy or woman) knew about sexuality, the better; certainly, it was greatly to be preferred that they do not discuss what they might have contrived to learn.

Even physicians appreciated the impropriety of talking about sex. When Dr. David Eder presented, in 1911, the first paper on clinical psychoanalysis to be read at a British Medical Association meeting, the chairman waited until Eder had finished and then stepped out of the room without a word, followed by the entire audience. Freud's books were treated as indecent. The 1913 English edition of *The Interpretation of Dreams* contains a message reading: ''Publishers Note. The sale of this book is limited to members of the Medical, Scholastic, Legal and Clerical professions.''

Such was the intellectual climate in which Ellis published his main works. It is to his everlasting credit that he was able to survive in such an atmosphere and that he was able to introduce fresh concepts about sexuality, concepts that are still very much alive today.

Edward Carpenter is, of course, less well-known than Ellis. He was born in 1844 and came from an educated middle-class family. He went to the university intending to become an Anglican clergyman and until he was nearly thirty his career developed along entirely conventional lines. He read mathematics and took a good degree, was made a fellow of his college, took holy orders, and became a curate under F. D. Maurice, the Christian socialist. By 1873 Carpenter felt that he could no longer continue in the church. He gave up holy orders, resigned his fellowship, and left Cambridge.

From this point on, Carpenter's life was more and more a complete rejection of Victorian conventions in politics, religion, and sex. He became a socialist, helped organize the Sheffield Socialist Society, and worked for a major change in the economy. Carpenter, too, was a vegetarian. More unusual, he admitted that he was homosexual and openly defended ''Uranians'' against social discrimination and legal punishment. Carpenter published many pamphlets on sex during the nineties: *Sex-love and its place in a Free Society, Marriage in a Free Society,*

*Woman and her place in a Free Society*. These titles indicate the center of his interests: he sought human freedom; when he wrote about sex he talked in terms of the liberation of the whole man, including his sexuality. In writings about sex, Carpenter tried to put aside conventional, institutional, and legal considerations and to deal with men and women simply as creatures having certain spiritual and physical needs, which could be either fulfilled or suppressed by their sexual relationships.

Carpenter's conclusions were based on intuition and occasional reference to secondary sources. They certainly could not be tested and hence never warranted the status of authority. Carpenter's most important contribution toward a modern understanding of sex was in the realm of social psychology. In discussing marriage, for example, Carpenter argued for a reasonable humane view that would recognize that love might end and would allow for an easier and honorable dissolution of the marriage contract. Here, he was far ahead of his time. In his book *Homogenic Love* (1896) and in *The Intermediate Sex* (1908), Carpenter was one of the first Englishmen to argue that homosexuality might be both natural and socially useful. Some of his arguments have become commonplace: one finds them, for instance, in the pages of the Wolfenden Report. Homosexuality, Carpenter said, might be an instinctive and congenital condition rather than a vice; in many cases the condition is ineradicable and the homosexual should therefore be accepted rather than exist under threat of punishment.

Havelock Ellis and Carpenter were, of course, exceptions in the discussion of sexuality in Victorian and Edwardian England. Many of their contemporaries reduced sexuality to the animal level, denied its role in the human situation, and continued to preach an overstrained, ascetic concept of sexual morality. Representative of this attitude were such educators as Edward Lyttelton and the Baden Powells, who sought to guide young people in their hours of recreation so that they would prefer healthful outdoor activities to the dubious pleasure of social dancing or to the even more dubious intellectual activity that might beguile them into vice. Lyttelton's books, *The Causes and Prevention of Immorality*

| THE LONELY ENGLISHMAN:
HAVELOCK ELLIS

*in Schools* (1887) and *The Training of the Young in the Law of Sex* (1900), treated sexuality as an unseemly and inconvenient itch that could be relieved only within the bonds of marriage.

By 1913 Lyttelton, as headmaster of Eton, could address the *Times* thus: "Those who are working and hoping, however feebly, to encompass the lives of our boys and girls with a wholesome atmosphere must know that in regard to sexuality two facts stand out. First, that in proportion as the adolescent mind grows absorbed in sex questions wreckage of life ensues. Secondly, that sanity and upright manliness are destroyed, not only by the reading of obscene stuff, but by a premature interest in sex matters, however it be excited." [20]

Lyttelton's struggle for preservation of the Victorian code of sexual morality was supported by such figures as Sir Robert Baden Powell, for many years leader of the Boy Scouts. He regarded sex as he regarded smoking and spectator sports—unhealthy practices that all good Scouts should avoid in order that they might become sturdy servants of the Crown. His sister, Agnes Baden Powell, wrote *A Handbook for Girl Guides* in cooperation with her brother. This work, too, warns adolescents against "secret bad habits" that lead to hysteria and lunatic asylums and serious illness. [21]

Thus one can see the conflict between two opposing ideas of sexuality, one denigrating and one dignifying, one repressive and the other liberating. This conflict continued throughout the early part of the twentieth century, and, in some social circles, still continues, only increasing in intensity as sexuality becomes a more openly acknowledged aspect of human experience.

Havelock Ellis fought a lonely fight to bring at least a measure of sexual emancipation to his England. It cannot be said that he succeeded. Old rigidities were only gradually eroded. World War I did something to emancipate women and sexuality in England, but the Victorian heritage continued to be a very strong influence as late as the 1920s and '30s. However rational and liberal Carpenter and Ellis might be on such issues as homosexuality, their influence did not manifest itself in changes of attitudes toward homosexuality. Indeed, the age of the Great Depression was too much involved with economic issues and projects for social reform to allow much attention to be given to sexual liberation. Pre-World War I socialism might talk of the woman question as one aspect of the social question and seek sexual freedom at the same time that it fought for economic justice, but the British Labour Party had no energy to spend on the "unleashing" of sexuality from Victorian fetters. After the failure of the great General Strike of the early 1920s, all Labour's attention had to be given to immediate issues of rebuilding trade union and party.

Havelock Ellis did not draw any of his followers into sex research. His methods were too literary and impressionistic to spark more conventional work with statistics and depth interviews. In one sense Havelock Ellis founded sexology in England and was its only really skilled practitioner. Whatever his deficiencies as a researcher, his attractively written work did, however, further the cause of sexual freedom.

I

*Three Contributions to the Theory of Sex* "stands, there can be no doubt, beside his [Freud's] *Interpretation of Dreams* as his most momentous and original contribution to human knowledge." [1] This book is Freud's major statement on the nature and development of sexuality in the human being. Yet, although psychoanalysis has become part of the background of the average educated man, most lay readers still have only a superficial understanding of Freud's concepts about sexuality.

It has been observed that the post-Darwinian world has invented two new religions: communism and psychoanalysis. If the first is distinguished by the enforcement apparatus of orthodoxy, the second may be characterized by the multiplication of heresies. Many of those "heresies," which are deviations from, or revisions of, Freudian theory, sprang from opposition to Freud's emphasis on the fundamental sexual basis for human behavior, both individual and social. When Jung, Adler, and Otto Rank—all notable among Freud's early disciples—came to differ with Freud and abandoned part of this theory, their differences were based on Freud's ideas about accepting the centrality of sex. Many other psychologists who have drawn inspiration from Freud have modified his theories drastically, again largely because they

FREUD AND
SEXUALITY

disagreed with Freud's excessive emphasis on the role of instinct, and particularly on the instinct of sex.

In these three essays, which constitute so important a part of Freud's work, he presents the core of his thesis that the neurotic person's experience is of such nature that he clings to the infantile aspects of his sexuality. Whereas the person who achieves a normal maturity passes through the phases of infantile sexuality and leaves most of these behind, the neurotic person finds it difficult to do so. He preserves infantile sex attitudes and behavior in many disguises, as it were, and often eventually reverts to some infantile form of sex expression. With this picture of human development in his mind, it was logical that Freud should focus his interest on sexual development in the child.

Most respectable people in Freud's time, however, regarded the child as a peculiarly pure creature. And no creature could be considered "pure" if it were tainted by sexuality. To be sure, the Christian infant might be redeemed from the world, the flesh, and the devil at his baptism, but by the end of the nineteenth century many people regarded that pledge as a mere ceremonial gesture. If any being on earth were innocent, it was the infant in his cradle or the toddler at his mother's knee. To suggest that the infant drew in libidinous delight with his mother's milk, and to assert that the toddler expressed enjoyment, anger, and many other pleasurable emotions in his refusal to be housebroken was, as Ernest Jones comments, "a calumny on the innocence of the nursery." [2]

Stendhal, however, in the autobiography he calls the *Life of Henri Brulard,* has given a vivid picture of himself as a young boy in his mother's arms, jealous of any other man who approached her, and most jealous of the man with the clearest legal right to do so. I quote from the book:

> *My mother, Madame Henriette Gagnon, was a charming woman, and I was in love with her. I hasten to add that I lost her when I was seven years old. In loving her at the age of perhaps six (1798), I had exactly the same character as*

*when in 1828, I loved Albertae de Rubempre with a mad passion. My way of starting on the quest for happiness had not changed at all in essentials, with this sole exception—that in which constitutes the physical side of love I was what Caesar would be, if he had come back to earth, with regard to the use of cannon and small arms. I should soon have learned and it would have changed nothing essential in my tactics. I wanted to cover my mother with kisses, and for her to have no clothes on. She loved me passionately and often kissed me—I returned her kisses with such ardor that she was often obliged to go away. I abhorred my father when he came and interrupted our kisses. I always wanted to give them to her on her bosom. Be so good as to remember that I loved her, in childbed, when I was barely seven.*[3]

But Stendhal was only beginning to be esteemed as a novelist when these three essays by Freud were first published in 1905, and the reader who was shocked by the theories of the relentlessly probing Viennese physician was equally disturbed by the French novelist.

Although Freud offered these theories to a public rather less officially inhibited than that of late Victorian England or the United States (which was shocked when President Theodore Roosevelt's daughter, Alice, was rumored to have smoked a cigarette), he was still addressing audiences, professional and lay alike, that had a deep-rooted fear of sexuality. For sex is the force in man that is hardest to control and therefore most in need of bridling.

Yet, in spite of all the changes in our mores that have occurred since the early 1900s, western society (and American in particular) still has this basic fear of sex. Nowhere perhaps has western society experienced more radical changes than in the United States; nowhere perhaps is sex a more marketable commodity, yet our very willingness to use sex as an adjunct to the sale of soap and automobiles may bear witness to our desire to make sexuality harmless by subduing it to the service of the marketplace. We have nominally liberalized our attitudes toward sex. Except for some survivals among inner-directed people who retain the stringent super-ego of earlier generations, sex expression has grown respectable. Men are supposed to be virile. Middle-class women are supposed to be sexually responsive and even enterprising. Our vocabularies have become more forthright. Our behavior is looser, although not necessarily more relaxed. Almost every phase of sexual behavior is now used as raw material by our novelists. Few words or acts are forbidden to the playwright. Even the producers of American films are increasingly ready to treat the "facts of life" with something approaching reality.

Yet, although American society does seem to have freed itself from some inhibitions and restrictions that prevailed in the past, residues of that past continue to affect our attitudes toward sex. To be sure, it is currently admitted that sex is a normal, even a worthy part of life. But if one listens to the "experts" on sex or reads the books that they produce for the layman, one becomes aware that their treatment of the subject is so superficial that relatively few people have a true understanding of sex.

Thus, even today many laymen may be unpleasantly surprised to hear that sexuality does not begin just at adolescence. Study of the child and the adolescent has become one of the central concerns of American psychologists, social psychologists, and sociologists alike. (In passing, one might note that it was G. Stanley Hall, an American pioneer in the study of the adolescent and his psychology, who brought Freud to America to lecture in 1909.) They are aware of the increase in the anxieties that young people experience as they move into puberty and through adolescence; they accept the adolescent as a seeker for a place in the world; they recognize the difficulties experienced by adolescents in dealing with problems of acquiring sexual maturity.

All these problems are involved with the adolescent's underlying concern, the search for a viable self, which Erik H. Erikson treats as the adolescent's special identity crisis.[4] Youth faces such crises in all societies, of course, but meeting them is especially difficult in societies that are changing as rapidly as ours. When Paul Goodman describes the state of *Growing Up Absurd,* he is concerned with the entire range of adolescent problems, but our dynamic society makes accommodations to sexual roles almost more difficult for young people than finding and carrying through vocational choices. Bruno Bettelheim, for example, thus sums up the differences between the sexual attitudes and prospects that people face in our technological society and those that grow out of the experiences of people living in a less complex world:

> *In societies in which technology has not yet affected the social conditions of women or their expectations, her sexual life is in far less conflict than in ours. It is still sufficient for her if her lover or husband enjoys sex with her. Since she feels that his enjoyment proves her a good woman, nothing stands in her way of enjoying herself; and, not worrying about whether she is frigid or has an orgastic experience, as likely as not she experiences orgasm. He, not obliged by older traditions or by any newer understanding to provide her with an orgastic experience, can enjoy himself, experience orgasm, and thus help her to experience it herself.*
>
> *In our society, the male youth needs as much as ever to have his virility attested by his sexual partner, and the female youth has a parallel need. But by now, the boy also needs to have his girl prove him a man by her so-called "orgastic experience," and the girl is even worse off. She not only has to prove him a man by making him experience orgasm; she must also prove her femininity by the same experience, because otherwise she must fear she is frigid. Sexual intercourse cannot often stand up to such complex emotional demands of proving so many things in addition to being enjoyable.* [5]

Since the external conditions of people's lives are so different from what they were in Freud's day, it is not unreasonable that psychotherapists should encounter today different problems with patients from those with which they would have dealt in Freud's time. The therapist still needs to be fully acquainted with the dynamics of sexual development, and Freud still offers the best description and analysis of those dynamics. Everyone who deals with young people—teachers, parents, social workers, administrators—or who wishes to increase his understanding of their elders (including himself) should also be familiar with Freud's analysis.

As previously mentioned, Freud's fundamental discoveries about sex have been emasculated. Although psychoanalysis has won particularly wide acceptance in the United States, that acceptance has come only as Freud's pessimism and his stress on libido theory have been deemphasized, if not repudiated, by the neo-Freudian groups, including the new existentialist school of psychotherapy. The rigid severity of Freud's concepts, his uncompromising readiness to follow them through to their logical conclusion, have been peculiarly disturbing to Americans. Dissatisfaction with the character of American civilization was limited to a few intellectuals in the prosperous 1920s. Then economic depression and war further tended to suppress Americans' willingness to face up to the dark message that was implicit in Freud's theory. As Jean-Paul Sartre writes:

*It is childhood, which traces out the blind alleys for prejudice; it is childhood which, feeling the curbs of its training, bucks like a snaffled colt and begins to resent belonging to a milieu. Today, psychoanalysis alone allows study to be made in depth of the process by which the child gropes his way in the dark and tries to act out, though he does not understand it, the social character which adults impose on him. It is psychoanalysis which shows if he is stifled in his role, whether he is trying to evade it or to assimilate himself completely to it. It is psychoanalysis alone that allows us to rediscover the whole man in the adult, that is to say, permits us to recognize not only his present determinations, but also the burden of his life-history.*[6] . . . *Certainly, for the majority of us, our prejudices, our viewpoints, our beliefs are "dead-ends"* because they were first experienced in childhood. *It is our childish blindness, our protracted daze which accounts, in part, for our irra-*

*tional reactions, the resistance we set up to reason. After all, just what was this fixation-making childhood if not a particular way of living the general interests of one's circle?* [7]

But modern Americans are committed to the belief that all things are possible, including escape from childhood. Many of them still believe that the child is a reservoir of goodness rather than an example of polymorphous sexual perversity. Hence, although Americans were quite prompt to see the potential usefulness of psychoanalytic treatment, they preferred other, more American-oriented theories—Rogers's client-centered therapy is a case in point. The growth of supportive and counseling therapy and the acceptance of selected portions of psychoanalytic ideas by many clergymen also indicate the kind of dilution that made Freud acceptable to a broad American public. [8]

Most of these approaches, it should be repeated, de-emphasize sex and particularly the influence of infantile sexuality. In his introduction to the first American translation of *Three Contributions to the Theory of Sex* (1910), Professor James Putnam pointed out the hostile attitude of his contemporaries toward the study of sexual behavior. Fifty years later, one must recognize that regardless of the impact of psychoanalytic thinking and despite the sexual sophistication to which many Americans dutifully pretend, a presumably informed public is still reluctant to approach problems of sexual behavior forthrightly and sensibly. Frank discussions of the nature and origin of sexual aberrations are still taboo, although there is a market for sensationalism and superficiality. Psychotherapists find an appalling ignorance about sexual deviations, and social scientists see this ignorance reflected in outbreaks of public hysteria. "Sex Fiend" in a headline sells papers, however mild the story inside; and even somber classics of fiction are made salable by "sexy" covers. The continued equation of sex with the forbidden and the dirty among so large a portion of the public leads one to think that the insights into the sexual behavior of man, which Freud presented in his work, are either not generally accepted or are badly misunderstood. The absence of serious sociological inquiry into variations of sexual behavior, and especially the lack of responsible original sociological studies on homosexuality,[9] for example, offer an interesting sidelight on the failure of social scientists to broaden their understanding of changes in the American character during recent decades.

These observations, incidentally, do not imply any denigration of post-Freudian psychoanalytic theory. On the contrary, Hartmann's ego-psychology, Anna Freud's theory of defense mechanisms, Fromm's cultural approach to the interpretation of psychoanalysis, and the insights of the existentialist school contribute significantly to a clearer understanding of the dynamics of neurosis and the requirements for its successful treatment. It is not easy to comprehend the so-called widening gap between what may be called "orthodox" Freudian theory and the modifications made by the "cultural" school. Both patients and psychoanalysts would benefit if greater emphasis was placed on the elements common to the theories of the principal psychoanalytic schools and less stress was put on their points of difference and divergence.

At the end of the first of the three essays on sexuality Freud says:

*If we are led to suppose that neurotics conserve the infantile state of their sexuality or return to it, our interest must then turn to the sexual life of the child, and we will then follow the play of influences which control the processes of development of the infantile sexuality up to its termination in a perversion, a neurosis or a normal sexual life.*[10]

The newer psychoanalytic schools, however, have tended to de-emphasize the role of infantile sexuality. And both theory and patients have suffered as a result. Certainly, in a rapidly growing society, where the individual must play more complex roles, and roles for which he is often exceedingly ill-prepared, a fresh orientation toward therapy may be needed in order to help patients handle the problems that they face. Society does indeed change the patient. Undoubtedly, the character of the symptoms from which contemporary patients suffer does differ from that found by Freud in the people who came to him for treatment. Many cases may not even be "clear-cut" in terms of their psychodynamics.

Borderline cases seem on the increase; borderline treatment, new orientations in therapy, new modifications of the relationship between patient and analyst may therefore be necessary.

Nevertheless, this does not diminish the significance of Freud's original observations on the libido theory, for example. Those who reject that offer no adequate substitute. Nor has any significant new theory on the development of sexuality been produced since Freud presented his basic concepts.

Similarly, although such studies as the Kinsey reports on sexual behavior and Irving Bieber's account of homosexuality [11] indicate that variations from conventionally acceptable sexual practices continue to play an important role in the lives of modern people, such studies of a strictly factual sort represent small progress in the theory of sexuality. And, indeed, even in the area of factual case study, we have not outmoded the basic nineteenth-century work of Krafft-Ebing (*Psychopathia Sexualis*), Hirschfeld (*Sexual Anomalies and Perversions*), and even Havelock Ellis (*The Psychology of Sex*), all of whom discussed sexual deviation in what was presumably a more prudish age.

Freud's own discussion of such aberrations as fetishism, sadism, and masochism is still of fundamental importance: "Fetishism" (1927), "A Child Is Being Beaten" (1919), "A Contribution to the Study of the Origin of Sexual Perversions" (1919), and "The Economic Problem of Masochism" (1924) are all classics. His treatment of male homosexuality may not be the final word on the subject. The absence of significant large-scale work on the etiology and treatment of homosexuality makes one wonder whether Freud and his contemporaries were not closer to a definitive interpretation of this phenomenon than are the modern analysts who stress the role of culture in its genesis. Freud's observations are still as relevant today as they were when first set down in his early work. In cases of inversion, as Freud called homosexuality, the individuals concerned have experienced a very early stage of fixation on their mothers and subsequently identified with them. This formulation of Freud still serves psychotherapists in dealing with certain homosexual patients and in interpreting homosexual problems.

Cultural conditions may indeed change and therefore significantly affect the sexual roles and expectations that people experience. But the sexual impulse and its varied implications, as stated by Freud, remain the same. This stress on the stability of sexual instincts may have confused and repelled many culturally oriented analysts during the last decades. They have undoubtedly detected the impacts of modern social and cultural changes upon both the adolescent and the adult, but in focusing upon these changes and in using them as the pivot about which to orient treatment, the culturalists have tended to ignore the basic dynamics that Freud developed on sexuality.

## II

Freud's contribution to the study of sexuality cannot be adequately discussed without considering the literary and cultural world of pre-World War I Vienna and, especially, without a look at some of the proceedings of the Vienna Psychoanalytic Society.[12] For—rather unlike the contemporary American picture—the pioneer generation of psychoanalysts tended to be genuinely cultivated persons as well as useful specialists in psychotherapy, and their work was influenced by the intellectual and artistic world in which they had their being. As Alfred Schick remarks, Viennese writers shared themes and insights with the psychologists. And the latter in their turn were stimulated by "the elements of magic and fairy tale in the old Baroque Theater" and particularly by the poets' use of symbol and hidden meaning.[13]

Each Wednesday evening Freud and his fellow members of the society would gather to read essays to each other and then to discuss the material that had been presented to them. It is particularly interesting to see how even this group of advanced thinkers tended to be relatively constricted in their attitudes toward sexuality. On the evening of November 11, 1908, for example, the society was talking about Albert Moll's

*The Sexual Life of the Child,* which several of the discussants regarded as an answer to Freud's *Three Essays.* Moll asserted that children had no awareness of, nor real curiosity about, sexual differences unless they were stimulated by indiscreet adults.[14]

During the exchange that followed, Eduard Hitschmann and Isidore Sadger raised the issue of cultural and class differences in attitudes toward sexuality. Sadger insisted that among Russian and Polish Jews, hysteria might be considered the statistical norm. Hitschmann noted that Jews seemed to have a particularly high incidence of neurotic ailments and "also that they have many more sexual experiences than others and—a fact that must be particularly emphasized—take them much more seriously."[15]

Fritz Wittels seems to take a particularly advanced position in the discussion, for he was one of the most progressive discussants at that meeting, advocating that children be told the "facts of life" promptly and clearly.

Freud, on the other hand, said, "As far as sexual enlightenment is concerned, Wittels's opinion differs perhaps from that of most of the group. It is still a question whether risks are not necessary for the development of personality. Someone has already pointed to the positive aspects of masturbation. Sexual enlightenment is something inorganic, as it were, something not provided for by nature."

Wittels was the chief speaker at the following meeting, on November 18, 1908, where sexual perversity was the topic of the evening. He observed that one of the reasons for calling perversions pathological was that they were ". . . so dreadful. This, however, is not a permissible basis for classification; disgust and dreadfulness are not objective symptoms. *Only that perversion is morbid that appears dreadful to the person who practices it. Accordingly, a masturbator may be ill and a licker of feces healthy."* (Author's italics.)

Wittels's own work was the evening's topic at the December 16, 1908, meeting when his book *Die Sexuelle Not* [16] was discussed by Professor Christian Freiherr von Ehrenfeld. The meeting was highly critical of Wittels's book, which developed two ideas: unrestrained sexual activity would spare man the damages that are brought on by suppression; the elimination of condemnation, moral and legal, is the only basis for a successful battle against venereal disease.

Ehrenfeld argues against Wittels's thesis that men should express their sexuality freely. Wittels replied to the contention that it is not possible for all people to satisfy their sexuality fully. In asserting the opposite, Wittels only wanted to say: "things cannot go on as they are today." How to bring about a change, he does not know. However, he considers it even more impossible that only the "most worthwhile" people should be given sexual freedom. "How is one to discover who are the most worthwhile people? Indeed, their worth starts with their fully satisfying their sexuality—or, under certain conditions, not satisfying it." [17]

Freud liked the book no better than Ehrenfeld did:

> *We distinguish . . . between a pathological process of repression and one that is to be regarded as normal. We try to replace the pathological process with rejection. This is also the only way open to society; society too must first revoke its suppression in order to be able to repudiate anew what had been suppressed, this time doing it in full consciousness and judiciously. That is why Freud strongly dislikes the motto of the book. . . . The terrifying picture that is painted of "libertinage" is an exaggeration: we can be sure that all the instincts would continue to exist alongside of liberty. Social need would take care of that. He is not inclined to regard the Caesars as mentally sick. It was their position that drove them to their excesses: we must not give people that unlimited sense of power. . . .* [18]

It is interesting to note that Jung reviewed Wittels's book very cordially: "I have not read a book on the problem of sexuality that so harshly and mercilessly tears to pieces our present-day morality, and yet in the main is so right; it is for just this reason that Wittels deserves to be read; but so do many others who write about the same topic. For it is not the single book that is of importance, but the problem common to them.'' [19]

In this instance, it is Jung who seems most ready to give sexuality its place in human existence and the Vienna analysts who feared that letting Eros loose would be equivalent to unleashing Chaos. Even in the privacy of professional discussion, the influence of conventional upbringing remained strong. Scientific detachment was one thing; no kind of human behavior should shock a psychoanalyst. But private life was another matter: there, even psychoanalysts preferred that sexuality express itself in conventional fashion. They were quick to proclaim personal distaste for the bizarre.

Although Krafft-Ebing, Havelock Ellis, and others had written about sexuality and sexual pathology, Freud's discussions of the unconscious and, particularly, the effect of sexual development on personality had far greater influence on American attitudes and behavior. Freud and Breuer's *Studies in Hysteria* had made some of these ideas available to nonprofessional readers as early as Freud's own later work, *Three Contributions to the Theory of Sex,* which offers a more concise statement of his views on sexuality than the *Studies in Hysteria* had done. But only after World War I did American readers really begin to be aware of Freud's work.[1]

No one can offer any detailed estimate of what popularization of psychoanalytic theory has done to liberate individuals [2]—particularly women—from Puritan anxieties about sex. The fact of psychoanalytic influence, however, cannot be doubted. Late nineteenth-century studies by sexologists, as well as those produced by sociologists, anthropologists, and psychologists working in the late 1920s and early 1930s, provided the setting that made it possible for Kinsey and the Sex Research Institute of the University of Indiana to carry on their inquiries during the 1940s. More important, perhaps, the earlier research and the increasing familiarity with Freudian theory created an intellectual climate in which readers would be prepared to accept—and to buy—

THE NEW
SEXOLOGISTS

Kinsey's massive reports on American sexual behavior. These reports in their tone supported what may have been a general impatience with the remnants of Victorian sexual mores—particularly among the increasing number of American young people who had been exposed to higher education. That serious studies of sexuality should be undertaken in the United States and that many people should be ready to read them (and perhaps even more people willing to read summaries of them) indicated that by the late 1940s once taboo topics could be dealt with in a soberly enlightening way. Each succeeding group of sex researchers has extended the study and broadened the understanding of sexuality, from Kinsey's statistical discussion of sexual outlets in the 1940s to Masters and Johnson's detailed study of human sexual response in the early 1960s.

Kinsey's research continues to be a monument to contemporary American sexology. He and his associates were the prime movers in altering popular notions about sexual behavior in America. Whatever criticisms may be made of the statistical evidence in the Kinsey reports, their pioneering presentation of the facts challenged and, almost at one stroke, changed many of the sexual inhibitions and prejudices that Americans still entertained.

An example of the direct and innovative attitude toward sexuality that the Kinsey research promoted can be found in an essay by Kinsey and his associates on normality and abnormality in sexual behavior:

*The non-specific nature of the basic sexual response of the human animal is especially apparent among more uninhibited groups in our American culture, and apparently in some other cultures. On this point we have data from some of the economically and educationally lowest groups with which we have worked, and also from certain of the intellectually and socially most assured segments of the population. In such groups a large number of children rate 2, 3, or 4 on the heterosexual-homosexual scale; and, what is most significant, a much larger number of the adults in such groups make both heterosexual and homosexual contacts throughout long periods of their lives. Out-side of our own culture, this same combination of heterosexuality and homosexuality in adult histories was apparently found in classic Greece, and it seems to be the picture in Mohammedan, Buddhist, and some other areas today.* [3]

In brief, Kinsey and his co-workers show concretely that human psychosexual behavior is rooted in a tendency to respond to stimuli. This response does not discriminate among sexual objects nor does it necessarily seek out particular channels of expression. Social pressures, and the conditioning they produce, determine which channels and objectives will be labeled *normal* and which *abnormal.*

This, the Kinsey studies observe, does not correspond to the Freudian picture of psychosexual development from indifferentiated responses through narcissistic and homosexual stages that lead to maturity, defined as concentration on genital heterosexual behavior. Nor does Kinsey's data support the interpretation of masturbation and homosexuality in an adult as the result of his fixation at some immature stage of development. The Kinsey Institute's preliminary examination of more than seven thousand life histories of men, and nearly as many histories of women, shows that only an exceedingly small portion ever passed through the hypothesized stages. Some children begin with an exclusively narcissistic interest in their own sexual responses; others, with exclusively heterosexual activities; still others, with exclusively homosexual play. The great majority, however, begin their sexual development by responding to any sufficient stimulus that may be available. This is exactly what might be expected from current knowledge about the structure and operation of the human sexual constitution.

Kinsey and his fellow students go on to maintain that the notion of the gradual social conditioning of an initial readiness to respond sexually satisfies the facts more simply than theories of pan-sexuality or of necessary polymorphous-perverse stages in psychosexual development. For the concept of necessary stages of development apparently implies that there are several different sorts of something called *sexuality,* and that the child's body somehow gives home-room to these impulses. Sexuality, in its biological simplicity, is a simple capacity to respond to any sufficient stimulus. "This is the picture of sexual response in the child and in most other younger mammals. For a few uninhibited adults, sex continues to remain sex, however they have it. But for most persons, a repetition of experience inevitably develops a preference for particular types of relationships. When, as in our society, there are tremendous rewards involved, and social reactions which may determine the life-time happiness or unhappiness of an individual, it is inevitable that certain types of sexual activity should predominate and become, in the thinking of the majority of persons, the natural, the normal, and the right kind of relationship."

This statement emphasizes the attitude of the new sexologists. They are relatively objective; they are not burdened by moral and cultural biases. They seek to observe sexual behavior by appropriate scientific means, whether in the laboratory or during careful interviews. Both observations and interviews are necessarily on selected subjects, to be sure; people who consider their sexual lives their own business, not to be discussed or made visible to strangers, cannot be part of the Kinsey Institute's sexual universe. The ability to get subjects, however, testifies to a loosening of taboos. (It may also bear witness to the antiseptic effect of scientific research—to which all things are pure—or to the American's historical tendency to consider regard for privacy as a form of snobbism.) The ability to get financing for the Kinsey Institute's work is even more eloquent testimony to the American respect for science. The work itself constitutes a breakthrough for sexology. Ever more it shows the beginning of a new attitude toward sexuality itself. One may be surprised that this socioscientific breakthrough should have occurred in a culture so often backward in its sexual attitudes. American culture certainly has not been flexible or even receptive in regard to sexuality. Sex might be recognized as necessary or even furtively acknowledged as pleasurable, but it was not respected. Even those who repeated the biblical injunction for man to multiply and replenish the earth may, one suspects, have wondered why the Lord in His wisdom gave His children such an undignified instrumentality for fulfilling His command. The United States has preserved, and not only in the hinterland, a great deal of Puritanism. American laws about sexual behavior are obsolete (even for the so-called Judeo–Christian civilization). When one compares these laws with the laws on sexual behavior in France and the Low Countries, for example, where the Napoleonic code still shows the far-sightedness of those who drafted the laws on order of the Emperor, one is struck by the appalling gap between what people do in fact and what the laws are supposed to punish.

Kinsey, however, changed at least the picture of sexuality that a scientific sexology presented. He disregarded moral evaluations of sexuality and thus was able to concentrate on the study of sexual behavior without having to deal with problems of sexual morality. His statement at the end of the article cited earlier is in a sense his program: ''In light of these accumulated data [the research at the Kinsey Institute], we must conclude that current concepts of normality and abnormality in human sexual behavior represent what are primarily moral evaluations. They have little if any biologic justification. The problem presented by the so-called sexual perversions is a product of the disparity between the basic biologic heritage of the human animal, and the traditional, culture codes.'' [4]

The importance of this statement cannot be stressed enough. Even now most European sexologists still adhere to the traditional notion of sexual perversion (Havelock Ellis, of course, was an exception). Most psychoanalytic schools, Freudian and neo-Freudian alike, still cling to moralistic concepts of sexual perversions. They continue to accept criteria of normality in sexual behavior, and consequently tend, in a rather high-handed and nonscientific way, to indoctrinate their patients with conventional concepts of sexuality. Unfortunately, few psychoanalysts will truly liberate their patients sexually, will try to make them at home or feel comfortable with their own sexual tastes. Instead too many analysts in dealing with sexual problems (or indeed with entire ranges of

patients' attitudes toward social issues) tend to reflect their own upbringing, social or religious, no matter how many years they have been
analyzed. Consequently, a conventional, often narrow suburban Middle
Western canon of attitudes is projected onto the patient's life-style. The
psychoanalyst thus becomes another servant of whatever Mrs. Grundy
may currently prescribe.

The situation is not too much better in Europe. World War II cut off
the line of distinguished German sexologists. There are really no inheri-
tors to the mantle of a Hirschfeld or a Krafft-Ebing. True enough, Germany had its Giese,[5] its von Gebsattel,[6] and its Schelsky,[7] but their
studies often contaminate scientific research with moralizing of one irrelevant sort or another. Schelsky's Soziologie der Sexualität (Sociology
of Sexuality), for example, definitely rejects the objective Kinsey
approach. He even talks about "democratic pluralism in sexuality,"
and thus, in fact, transports political concepts into the discipline of
sexology, which has long been muddled by concepts more proper to
morality. Although cultural facts are important in the interpretation of
sexual behavior, they should not be taken as sufficient criteria of what
sexuality is and how, in fact, it is expressed. It has become clear that in
order to deal with sexuality as a total experience, it is necessary to
approach sexuality objectively, with the minimum of prejudgments and
with a clear awareness of our own special biases, whether of personal
preference or social purpose. Some students have approached the material in this spirit. For example, as early as 1923 Scheler was describing
perversions as the "other sexuality." [8] And Annemarie Wettley tries to
establish that we are indeed moving away from the pathological emphasis of earlier sexological studies to a more existential approach to sexuality.[9]

Even existential psychoanalysts, interested as they are in the varieties
of sexual behavior, have not been able to divest themselves from
preconceived notions on perversions and on sexuality in general.[10] Still
we also know, especially as the result of Kinsey's findings, that obscure
psychoanalytic studies on the varieties of sexuality can no longer be dis-

missed as isolated instances that do not reflect the culture. We should certainly have learned by now that we can no longer take certain notions about sexuality and sexual behavior for granted. Everything is in flux. No longer can we feel safe from surprise by our sexual researchers. And here lies the major difference between the studies of Hirschfeld *et al.* and the Kinsey sexologists. The latter have exerted a profound impact upon sexual attitudes in our culture. There seems little doubt that students like Hirschfeld did not exert so far-reaching an influence. Havelock Ellis was respected and read in England, but principally by upper-class intellectuals, whose sexual attitudes always had been flexible and liberal, out of the ordinary. They needed no Havelock Ellis or Hirschfeld to liberate their sexuality.

The result of sexological study has penetrated social strata below the confined circle of medical men and well-informed literati. By now, studies of the Kinsey sort have profoundly influenced the attitudes of contemporary Americans. As Father John M. Culkin, director of communications at Fordham University, said, "What was once the realm of private knowledge had become public knowledge and . . . perhaps there's too much honesty but there's no doubt that these things have become part of the public domain." [11] Thus, the major difference between sexologists today and the early workers in the field is the altered social climate in which they work. Once Havelock Ellis was prosecuted for obscenity because his *Studies in the Psychology of Sex* was so shocking. Now, the Kinsey Reports become best-sellers and are abridged and simplified for hurried or uneducated readers (some of whom may, of course, have been disappointed in their expectations of suitably disguised pornography). The public today can see a spade called a spade: it need not know Latin to follow Krafft-Ebing's case histories. The mass media have found that they can profit by publicizing serious studies of sexuality in some diluted form or other. They may continue paying lip service to "love," "personal commitment," and "the need for stable family relations," but their pictures show not only luscious young women but also men of an all but caricatured virility.

And all their advertisers have discovered that nothing sells like sex.

Obviously, contemporary sexologists still have the task of helping to remove many prejudices about sexuality. These have burdened mankind for centuries and may well continue to trouble his life. But the sexologists are continuing to bring the facts of sexual experience into the light. In order to discover these facts, students of sexuality have had to become aware that they, too, might have been worshipping the ideal of the tribe, accepting unconsciously their culture's preconceived notions about sexuality. Objectivity in this field is not easy, but objectivity is the scientists' obligation and the sexologist considers himself a scientist.

While the contemporary European sexologists continued to concern themselves with developing Hirschfeld and Krafft-Ebing, with describing and explaining so-called pathological aspects of sexuality, Kinsey and other American sexologists have tried to dismiss myths and taboos about sexuality by objectively reporting the behavior of individuals who were normal, who lived in the ordinary world, not the insane asylum or the jail. Kinsey's findings about the sexual behavior of ordinary Americans, male and female, cover *all* areas of human sexual behavior.[12] Thus, they provide a rich source of information about masturbation among contemporary adult men and women. They depict class differences in sexual expression. They offer statistical information about premarital and extramarital intercourse.

The new sexologists have a distinct advantage in being able to work in a social environment where sexuality is seen as part of our total life experience and not something restricted to the bedroom. For the first time in history perhaps, we may see sexuality not merely as an instinct but as part of our consciousness, our life-style, our philosophy of life, our whole existence in short. A distinguished French philosopher, Paul Ricoeur, sees many contemporary problems stemming from the disappearance of the *sacred* from contemporary sexuality.[13] Where once Helen of Troy, or the goddess Aphrodite, personified the terror in sexuality, its power to make people break all social rules, to destroy others and themselves, now some shadowy image on the television or movie screen promises happiness if we use the proper toothpaste, the collector of sexological statistics tells us that $\alpha$ percent of all men below the age of nineteen have had intercourse with their aunts, and the adolescent girl carries birth-control pills along with her loose change and hair curlers. The change from sexuality as sacred to mundane may be felt as a loss, but even Ricoeur acknowledges that the change had to occur.

In the coming decades, sexologists must face the question of the relation between marriage, which Ricoeur calls the greatest risk in our society, and sexuality. In short we must be less concerned about labeling the varieties of sexual behavior as normal and abnormal and more concerned with sexuality as an aspect of the human adventure—which may lead to joy and fulfilment or to boredom and violence or to that "quiet desperation" that Thoreau found to be most men's lives.

# part 2

## THE VARIETIES OF SEXUALITY

Any discussion of the nature and origin of the sexual varieties necessarily raises two questions: What is sexual normality? How are concepts of normality related to their cultural context? Currently, most sociologists and psychoanalysts would agree that what is regarded as normal sexual practice in one culture may be considered a perversion in another. They would also agree that it is extremely difficult to define sexual normality even within the limits of a specific culture and its social structure.

Since it is thus difficult to define the norm, defining perversion,* departure from the norm, presents that much more of a problem. Freud has written: "In no normal person does the normal sexual aim lack some designable perverse element, and this universality suffices in itself to prove the expediency of an opprobrious application of the name perversion. In the realm of the sexual life one is sure to meet with exceptional difficulties, which are at present unsolvable, if one wishes to draw a sharp line between the mere variations within physiological

---

* I have used the word perversion throughout in a clinical sense. No judgment is involved. As a matter of fact the word perversion as such is rapidly disappearing from the psychoanalytic vocabulary.

THE ORIGINS OF
SEXUALITY

limits and morbid symptoms." [1] Nevertheless, it is possible to draw a distinction, although it may have somewhat irregular contours. Warner Muensterberger comes closest to a workable definition when he observes that most perverse sexual expression avoids natural sexual contact and hence fails to meet genital demands in a genital way. (*Perverse* is used here rather than *perverted,* which seems to have a more judgmental quality.)

Psychoanalysts generally accept two phenomena as the causes for the emergence of perverse sexual behavior: the castration complex and ego splitting. Robert Bak relates ego splitting and perversion in terms of the young child's attempt to deal with intensely destructive wishes directed toward the parent of the opposite sex. To preserve this person (for the child believes his wishes can kill) ". . . an identification with the hated objective is made as a defense against the aggressive wishes. . . . In perversions the ego undergoes a split instead of utilizing repression and other defenses against the representatives of the fixated drives." [2]

W. H. Gillespie points out that in terms of castration we are dealing with "a specific modification of castration anxiety, determined in its form by earlier, pregenital, and especially oral developments." [3] Melanie Klein suggests that the splitting phenomenon is characteristic of an early stage of ego development, when ego organization is still imperfect and disintegration can easily occur. Gillespie carries Klein's concept further to find a significant difference between perversion on one hand and neurosis and psychosis on the other. By utilizing the mechanism of splitting the ego, the patient is able to avoid psychosis. For one part of his ego can accept reality and function within it. To quote Gillespie again: ". . . the split allows his mind to function on two levels at once—the pregenital, oral-sadistic level corresponding to psychosis, and the phallic level, where his conscious mental content bears so much resemblance to the repressed content of the neurotic." [4]

Although we have these clinically useful notions about the origins of perversion, students of human behavior continue to be concerned with the concept of sexual normality. Sidney Axelrad has suggested that the criterion of psychosexual normality be the individual's capacity for post-ambivalent relationship rather than the mere statistical norm of the culture in which perverse behavior appears. He thus implies that certain acts are absolutely perverse, whatever their acceptability in a given society. Alexrad thus rejects Kinsey's conclusions as well as those of George Devereux, who has previously suggested that some specific expression of the sexual drive might be condoned, or even accepted, by one culture whereas it was considered perversion, to be rejected or perhaps punished, by another. Muensterberger takes an ambiguous stand on the issue of criteria for normality. He observes that both sadism and homosexuality are normal among the Korakis of New Guinea and the Big Nambas of New Hebrides. Nevertheless, he writes, although ". . . these practices belong to the standard cultural organization, they have to be labeled perversions because the aggressive discharge and pleasure are *experienced genitally and through ejaculation.*" [5]

If certain kinds of sexually involved behavior are to be considered perverse only in the context of their acceptability in a given culture, one may well raise another issue, that of the historical development of attitudes toward perversion and the subsidiary point of the impact of those attitudes on behavior. Axelrad observes that the dominance of Judeo-Christian morality has tended to suppress the institutions that created channels for socially acceptable expression of what western culture now labels perversions, but in fact are *mere* variations of sexuality. In consequence, Axelrad argues, pregenital drives have been inhibited, the role of magic has been diminished, and ego strength has risen, along with men's capacity to master narcissistic injuries.

Axelrad's conclusions are suggestive, but they also raise certain questions. The concepts of Judeo-Christian morality label "perverse" and even "unnatural" any sexual behavior that is not strictly interpersonal and genital; even heterosexual oral contact is considered abnormal. We read about "unnatural acts" and even "unnatural vice." The behavior cloaked in such euphemisms is entirely natural, however, since from the scientific point of view whatever occurs in nature is natural, however unusual it may appear.

As perverse behavior seems to be thus native to man, one may question both the effectiveness of Judeo-Christian morality in inhibiting it and the psychological usefulness of the form which that inhibition has taken. For example, the role of magic in modern life has certainly changed, but one has good reason to wonder whether the total amount of magic practices has really diminished. Few philosophers in our society practice necromancy, as Plotinus and his Alexandrian followers are said to have done, but the popularity of certain types of "horror" films —*Donovan's Brain,* for instance—indicates that many contemporary people at least wish that the dead could be revived (the "Zombie" theme) and reveal secrets. And who that passes a store window bearing a painted palm and the legend "Indian Reader and Advisor" can say that fortune-telling no longer flourishes, although Judeo-Christian morality condemns it as all but sacrilegious.

Again, Judeo-Christian morality scarcely sanctions sadomasochism, yet both the Marquis de Sade and Leopold von Sacher-Masoch grew up in Christian countries. Christian churches do not all disapprove such "mortification of the flesh" as wearing hair shirts and even tight chains to break and irritate the skin. Self-flagellation was an accepted form of Christian penance during the Middle Ages. Flagellation is still ceremonially practiced in Spanish-Indian communities in our own southwestern states (not with the sanction of the contemporary Catholic Church, it should be said). And Britain has a Corpun Society dedicated to the preservation of corporal punishment as a method of classroom discipline. When a series of violent crimes shocks a community, we hear demands for the revival of flogging as a punishment and the state of Delaware retained an official whipping post far into the twentieth century. Nor has the beating of suspects and the "roughing up" of arrested persons ceased to be a rather routine part of police procedure in many cities.

Judeo-Christian morality may indeed have caused other perversions or varieties of sexuality to become internalized and their expression to be inhibited. Clinical experience, however, may well cause the psychotherapist to wonder whether external pressures of this sort may not have worked more injury than is commonly realized. Furthermore, one may doubt whether the introduction of Judeo-Christian morality and its reinforcement by legal sanctions have indeed operated to decrease the total quantity of expressed perversion or even sexuality *per se*.

To be sure, social institutions no longer make at least some sexual perversions socially respectable. We do not subject young men to painful initiation rites as did the Plains Indian tribes—although youths have been severely injured as a result of initiation into college fraternities. We do not give transvestism and male homosexuality formal social sanction as the Plains Indians did when they institutionalized those perversions in the form of the *berdache,* the man who lived as a woman in all respects except that he was often better at the strictly feminine crafts such as quill embroidery. We no longer wear ''mourning rings,'' which enclose bits of hair from the beloved dead, but this custom nevertheless continued into the nineteenth century. And who that is familiar with the popular literature of sentimentality—all antiseptically pure of contamination by anything overtly sexual—does not know how suitors begged the girls they were courting for locks of their hair.

But, one may repeat, the attenuation of perversions and the absence of socially approved channels for its overt expression does not necessarily mean that less perversion exists. People who have a psychological need to express themselves sexually in some odd manner can find ample opportunity to gratify that need. Secret clubs for the practice of perversion have undoubtedly existed for many years and probably continue to exist, although we know little about them; after all, such organizations would be accessible for study only to peculiarly qualified researchers. But opportunity to engage in way-out sexual behavior is not restricted to those who have access to select secret clubs. Certain publications print advertisements through which those interested in the practice of perversion can communicate with each other. Krafft-Ebing noted the existence of such ''agony columns'' in Germany as early as 1886, when his

*Psychopathia Sexualis* appeared. Currently, similar advertisements appear in both Canadian and United States journals.[6]

If we look back in time a little, we see that perversion did not cease to be practiced in modern Europe merely because the prevailing moral code bore heavily on pregenital sexual expression. When we look at nineteenth-century England, for example, we learn that sadomasochistic behavior was known as *le vice Anglais* on the Continent.[7] Flogging was a common punishment in both the British army and navy during the eighteenth and far into the nineteenth century. Flogging was also the accepted means of school discipline, and in stories about British public schools (even Dr. Arnold's reformed Rugby) one reads how boys were beaten with rods not only by their teachers but also by older boys who, under the honor system, were charged with keeping their juniors in order. Elsewhere, we learn that George IV was a regular patron of the salon of a Mrs. Collet where the first flagellating machine, "Berkeley Horse," was used on desirous visitors.[8] The poet Swinburne seems to have acquired a taste for being flogged as a boy at school and wrote a number of poems glorifying the birch and the flogging block.[9]

The basic reason for the British emphasis on sadomasochism would require prolonged research by a sociologist who had both a historical sense and a good deal of psychoanalytic training. Whether *le vice Anglais* corresponds to a social reality or merely reflects the tendency to charge one's own vices to one's neighbors would also bear investigation. After all, the English and the Italians called syphilis "the French disease."

Certainly neither sadomasochism nor homosexuality is confined to one country any more than perverse behavior is limited to one sex.[10] In Imperial Germany, fetishism and flagellation had a very great appeal, as the works of Krafft-Ebing and Hirschfeld give evidence. Homosexuality, overt and latent, can be seen in many aspects of German life long before the rise of Nazism. The tradition of wandering and comradeship, which goes back to the roving students and journeymen of the Middle Ages, has a striking homosexual component. Youth movements, a German development of the Romantic period, continued through the nine-teenth century and into the 1920s and 1930s. These, too, served to focus much unconscious homosexuality.[11]

Armies tend to bring out both sadomasochistic and homosexual trends in both officers and men, and Germany, or rather Prussia, has been highly militarized since the mid-eighteenth century. In the army of Imperial Germany, homosexuality was rampant, although the notorious von Eulenberg case did not involve an officer but a high-ranking civil servant, a friend of Kaiser Wilhelm himself.[12]

The psychoanalyst who studies the Nazi movement can see many of its practices as permitting, or even encouraging, latent perverse tenden-cies to express themselves. Uniforms, for example, have a definite fe-tishistic appeal and even before the Nazis took over the government, they had added a variety of uniforms to those officially available. Both in practice and in theory, the Nazi movement gave its members opportu-nity to engage in such perverse practices as fetishism and flagellation, which had become almost fashionable in certain Berlin circles during the 1920s. To discuss sadism (and masochism) in Nazi concentration camps is beyond the scope of this introduction. Dr. Elie A. Cohen, who has made a careful study of the problem, concludes that most members of the SS, the Nazi elite guard, were psychologically normal, criminals whose behavior may be hard to distinguish from perversion, but who cannot be categorized as perverse, governed by their pregenital sexual drives.[13]

Again, homosexual behavior was quite evident in Nazi groups, al-though Hitler himself disapproved and considered notorious and overt homosexuality a useful reason for treating Ernst Roehm as a corrupter of German youth who therefore deserved to be shot.[14]

The therapy of homosexuality,[15] like that of other sexual varieties, is still highly problematic. Very few, if any, positive results have been achieved, and on the whole the prognosis is very poor. Perhaps this therapeutic ineffectiveness is to be attributed, at least in part, to the meager attention that contemporary scholars have devoted to the varie-

| THE ORIGINS OF
SEXUALITY

ties of sexual behavior. The works of Krafft-Ebing, Hirschfeld, and Havelock Ellis are by now outdated. Current studies, even when they do seek to relate the psychological and sociological aspects of the problem of perversion, tend to be somewhat sketchy and superficial.[16] The contemporary study of the sexual varieties awaits its Kinsey. The psychotherapist may be encouraged by the appearance of an increasing number of studies of homosexuality, even though this body of work still lacks needed scope and depth and is too subjective, and therapist and social scientist alike still need more far-reaching studies on other phases of sexual behavior.

Bisexuality continues to intrigue men and women in our contemporary society. Today when crises in sexual identity are fairly pronounced and continuously and openly discussed, many persons don the mask of bisexuality in order to avoid their heterosexual or homosexual drives. Lay persons often assume that the majority of sexologists, psychologists, biologists, and psychoanalysts accept the concept of bisexuality. Nothing could be further from the truth.

In tracing the origin of the concept of bisexuality it becomes clear that the term was used to explain sexual inversion or homosexuality. In other words, those laymen who maintain that bisexuality is an actual biological phenomenon are primarily latent and repressed homosexuals and perhaps some overt homosexuals. Bisexuality, whether as a concept or a practice, rarely holds any attraction for the functioning heterosexual.

Discussions of bisexuality often attribute the concept to Freud. However, it was the French writer E. Gley who suggested in 1884 [1] that bisexuality might account for inversion or homosexuality. Freud himself owed the idea of bisexuality to his friend Wilhelm Fliess, as Ernst Kris writes in his introduction to *The Origins of Psychoanalysis:*

*Freud's advance from the study of dreams and parapraxes to the further development of his sexual theory was facilitated by an idea that he took over from Fliess. This*

THE MYTH OF
BISEXUALITY.

*was the significance of bisexuality. In the introduction to his 1897 monograph, Fliess, after proclaiming the existence of both male and female periods, went on to develop the theme of constitutional bisexuality. This problem played an important role in the exchange of ideas between the two men. Freud was fascinated by it, and quickly adopted Fliess's idea that the theory of bisexuality was capable of making an important contribution to the understanding of the neuroses.* [2]

The majority of Fliess's contemporaries used bisexuality as a link to sexual inversion. They also linked bisexuality to normal sexual behavior; consequently they saw inversion as the result of a disturbance in development. G. Herman was convinced that "masculine elements and characteristics are present in every woman and feminine ones in every man." [3] Krafft-Ebing stated that a great number of observations "prove at least the virtual persistence of this second centre [that of the subordinated sex]." [4] The views of the philosopher Otto Weininger, who developed the concept of bisexuality in his book *Sex and Character,* contributed to the emergence and acceptance of the idea of bisexuality. It is also interesting to note that Freud links bisexuality to the residues of a physical hermaphroditism:

> . . . *it appears that a certain degree of anatomical hermaphroditism occurs normally. In every normal male or female individual, traces are found of the apparatus of the opposite sex. These either persist without function as rudimentary organs or become modified and take on other functions. These long-familiar facts of anatomy lead us to suppose that an originally bisexual physical disposition has, in the course of evolution, become modified into a unisexual one, leaving behind only a few traces of the sex that has become atrophied.* [5]

Sandor Rado in "A Critical Examination of the Concept of Bisexuality" [6] also examines the origin of the concept of bisexuality. He remarks that in the middle of the nineteenth century it was discovered that the urogenital systems of the two sexes derive from a common embryonic origin. The subsequent finding that this *Uranlage* (primitive structure) contained cellular material of both gonads [7] gave it the label of *hermaphroditic*. This in turn opened the door to all kinds of indiscriminate speculations on bisexuality and Rado writes that, as a result, Krafft-Ebing, for example, developed the neuropsychological aspects of bisexuality into the following theory:

> . . . *since the peripheral part of the sexual apparatus is of bisexual disposition, this must be true of the central part as well. Thus one must assume that the cerebrum contains male and female centers whose antagonistic action and relative strength determine the individual's sex behavior.* [8]

Homosexuality results from the victory of the wrong center. Krafft-Ebing realized that hermaphroditic developmental abnormalities of the genitals rarely are associated with homosexuality. Consequently, he went on to make the further assumption that the central part of the sex system is autonomous and therefore independently subject to developmental disturbances. Not a trace of neurological evidence was available then or now to validate Krafft-Ebing's chain of hypotheses. Nevertheless, many followed blindly in accepting his notion of bisexuality, among them Havelock Ellis and Magnus Hirschfeld.

Although Freud did indeed work with the concept of bisexuality, it was only with reservations, and Rado points out very clearly what these reservations and limitations are:

> *In the desire to remain free and unbiased in the evaluation of his findings, Freud intentionally kept himself apart from the other medical sciences. He was obliged however to use as points of orientation a few of the basic assumptions of biology, and it was as one of these that he introduced into psychoanalysis the concept of bisexuality. This borrowed concept, formulated as a general characteristic of every human individual, came to play so important a role in psychoanalytic theory that younger men in the field dealt with it, not as a postulate or convenient frame of reference for interpretation, but as an established fact. Freud himself had no*

*pretentions on this score: as recently as 1933 he reiterated that he had "merely carried over the notion of bisexuality into mental life. . . ." [9]*

Even more important, Freud makes it abundantly clear in his *New Introductory Lectures* that he himself is dubious about the concept of bisexuality:

> *Even in the sphere of human life you soon see how inadequate it is to make masculine behavior coincide with activity and feminine with passivity. . . . If you now tell me that these facts go to prove precisely that both men and women are bisexual in the psychological sense, I shall conclude that you have decided in your own minds to make "active" coincide with "masculine" and "passive" with "feminine." But I advise you against it. It seems to me to serve no useful purpose and adds nothing to our knowledge. [10]*

Contemporary biologists go further than Freud. They reject the theory of bisexuality outright. As F. R. Lillie writes: "Sex of the gametes and sex in bodily structure are two radically different things." [11] Rado puts it as follows: "Using the term bisexuality in the only sense in which it is biologically legitimate, there is no such thing as bisexuality in either man or in any other of the higher vertebrates. In the final shaping of the normal individual, the double embryological origin of the genital system does not result in any physiological duality of reproductive functioning." [12]

It has been observed earlier that wherever bisexuality is mentioned or introduced into psychological discussion, it comes within the context of homosexuality. For any normally functioning heterosexual male the question of bisexuality is as academic as the question of homosexuality. Reflections on a general male capacity to function sexually with both men and women make interesting table talk. Such formulations may foster slick generalizations (if not rationalizations) but they serve no serious purpose. Freud's position on this point is again perfectly clear, when he writes, in "Analysis Terminable and Interminable," "A man's heterosexuality will not tolerate homosexuality, and *vice versa.*" [13] (Author's italics).

Freud's statement, in effect, destroys any tenable argument for the idea of bisexuality. It becomes clear in the course of psychotherapy that the modes of sexual adjustment in which the patient must operate are either heterosexual or homosexual. This either/or approach is particularly rejected by people who are unwilling to face up to their sexuality as part of their whole being; and therapists should emphasize that the patient should abandon the concept of sex as a collection of "partial instincts" and see sexual behavior as a total reaction of one human person to another. This point has been especially stressed by existential psychotherapists. [14]

Leon Salzman in his essay "Latent Homosexuality" points to another aspect of this problem:

>In therapy, so-called "latent" homosexual attitudes are often described as appearing in the course of psychoanalytic work. At these times, abortive attempts to relate to people of the same sex or to a therapist of the same sex are viewed as evidence of latent homosexuality. Such activity may actually be indicative of growing capacities and desires for more tender and intimate participation of a nonsexual nature. [15]

In terms of sexual identity, the concept of bisexuality is more than outmoded; it may even be dangerous. For many patients cling to the concept of bisexuality *in order* to avoid coming to terms with their own sexuality. In an open society like ours, where it becomes increasingly difficult for the individual to wear a mask and where pressure for assertion of sexual identity is far greater than, say, at the beginning of the twentieth century, confronting one's sexuality, whatever it may be, becomes a crucial matter. Bisexuality as a *mask* might have worked fairly well in the nineteenth century. Then, in most cases, it served to disguise the overt or repressed homosexuality of a given individual. Three examples may be cited. John Addington Symonds, a British literary critic and historian, married and had four children. Yet the emo-

| THE MYTH OF
BISEXUALITY

tional side of his sexual life was totally homosexual. Oscar Wilde was married and had children. The mask of bisexuality worked here only to a certain extent, and it finally crumbled completely. André Gide married, probably out of respect for the customs of his time. He, too, was finally unable to withstand the homosexual orientation in his life.[16] Bisexuality also served Marcel Proust, who made use of it both in his personal life and in his literary works. As Milton Miller writes:

*Proust was struggling to express his concept of bisexuality in a literary way at around the same time Freud was working out, in his own mind, the possible universality of bisexuality and its role in neuroses. . . . How much of Proust's interest in demonstrating the bisexual nature of many of his characters was due to his reading of psychiatric or medical literature is not known. However, we can see from his novel that bisexuality was often a key which led back to the nostalgic past, always tempting and never fully satisfying.*[17]

To repeat, three of these men married and, initially, they led perfectly normal heterosexual lives, and their behavior responded to the expectations of their culture. Overt homosexuality was still heavily censured; hence the mask of bisexuality offered useful social shelter.

In our time, when the question of sexual identity has become increasingly crucial, it might be expected that any concept of *confused* sexual identity, that is, the concept of bisexuality, should be closely scrutinized. It is obvious that our patients (and people who are not in therapy) are now, thanks to Freud and Kinsey, forced into an open confrontation with sexuality.

Under these circumstances, it also becomes clear that using the concept of bisexuality as a means to sit on the fence and leave sexuality undetermined is no longer useful in the process of psychotherapy. It tends to confuse patients who are unable to find a mode of sexual adjustment because of their constant flirtation with either heterosexuality or homosexuality.

Men who, in their twenties, deceived themselves into belief that they could reconcile their heterosexual and homosexual drives on the basis of a bisexual adjustment often in their forties find themselves caught in a severe sexual crisis. The homosexual tendency can no longer be repressed, nor can it be acted out as a mere incidental diversion. Consequently, the very basis of their lives is threatened. Their wives and children suffer in the process, and since they are often too old for any significant depth analysis, they find themselves at the end of their rope.

No stable sexual identity or significant sexual adjustment can be achieved where the patient has not fully worked through his sexual situation. We may very well still be suffering from some type of reaction-formation to Freudian therapy and the distorted notion that orthodox Freudian analysts placed too much emphasis on sexuality. The failure of neo-Freudian therapy by and large to come to terms with problems of sexual identity accounts for this.

Since it has become evident that there is no biological evidence for bisexuality and that any proof of such a phenomenon in psychoanalytic terms is highly questionable, it would be extremely helpful to patients and therapists alike if we dispelled the myth of bisexuality. In the next decades, the confrontation with sexuality *per se* will even become more important both in the psychoanalytic process and in the outside world. Such a confrontation with one's sexuality requires clear-cut definitions and approaches to what constitutes human sexuality. The contemporary patient who is struggling with both his sexual identity and an identity crisis at large does not require the mask of bisexuality. He needs, rather, to commit himself to making a genuine sexual choice.

I
"Sex" has stopped being a nasty word in America. We can talk about good sexual performance in mixed company in some quite conventional circles almost as freely as we discuss good professional performance. Certainly, it is currently far more socially acceptable to be permissive about sex than to be iconoclastic about religion or even critical about political institutions. Nevertheless, American law continues to treat homosexuals in an almost medieval manner; the homosexual is harried by the police on occasion; in some states in the union (Colorado, Georgia, and Nevada) homosexuality may be penalized by life imprisonment (a punishment that gives prime opportunity for continuing the offense). And that faceless generality, "the public," although it may be somewhat better informed than it was a generation ago, continues to be intrigued by what was called *unnatural* vice long after Victorian America had stopped disguising *legs* as *limbs*. Näiveté and prurient curiosity alike have been increased, or even pandered to, by novels, plays, and sensationally advertised books that purport to be—and sometimes even are—serious psychological studies of homosexuality.

When homosexuality is dealt with in scientific sobriety, it is generally treated from the psychoanalytic point of view: What in their indi-

HOMOSEXUALITY: A
CONTEMPORARY VIEW

vidual experience makes some people become homosexuals? How, when they do follow this path, do they behave? How can they bring themselves either to change their behavior or to become better adjusted to their lives if they do not change? The psychotherapist is not generally interested in the sociological aspects of homosexuality, however. The sociologist, on the other hand, either is not interested in the problem or, if he is, often tends to concentrate on collecting data to show that the practice of homosexuality is (or is not) increasing or is (or is not) so common as to constitute at least a statistical norm. The relationship between contemporary manifestations of homosexuality in America and the contemporary development of American society attracts appallingly little attention from social scientists. And this, of course, is consistent with prevailing patterns of timidity: many a modern sociologist is a collector of facts frightened by the specter of a generalization, let alone a theory.

This discussion approaches homosexuality from the sociological rather than the psychoanalytic point of view. It sees the increase of homosexuality in the United States as part of the existential situation generated by a swiftly changing society, which often seems to exist for, rather than to be served by, the technology it is producing. In this society men are and even feel themselves to be more and more alone.

In spite of increased information, the stereotype of the homosexual still colors people's ideas. The "gay" boy is effeminate in manner: he knows more about dressing women than any woman does—and, using his knowledge to make women look grotesque, so states his hostility to the sex. He inhabits the elegant, small art galleries, the showrooms of the interior decorators who fill the rooms of people too unimaginative to furnish their own houses, the expensive florist shops, the theater, and other enterprises that purvey costly amenities to those too devoted to (and successful in) the pursuit of money to develop any really independent manner of adorning their lives.

And, of course, the homosexual is neurotic. His neurosis, the stereotype continues, confines him to his peculiar fields of activity. However, a study by Dr. Evelyn Hooker involving a group of thirty heterosexuals and a group of thirty homosexuals presents some very interesting findings. Each member of each group was paired with respect to age, educational level, and I.Q. with a member of the opposite group. All were given a battery of projective tests, including the Rorschach, on the basis of which they were then given blind ratings as to adjustment. Later efforts by judges to determine which member of each pair was the homosexual resulted in neither judge scoring better than chance. Although Dr. Hooker is very hesitant to ascribe too much significance to her findings because both the control group (consisting of an equal number of heterosexuals) and the experimental group (consisting of an equal number of homosexuals) were highly selected, it would appear that, if one is to consider the Rorschach a valid criterion for determining adjustment, there is no inherent linkage between pathology and homosexuality.

Of course, it might be difficult for an active homosexual to maintain the posture of a good family man as is required of the contemporary American politician. It is also difficult for a divorced heterosexual to maintain that posture. The promiscuous homosexual who compulsively prowls the streets and haunts public rest rooms may indeed be the prisoner of his neurosis. But so is the miser, the drug addict, the alcoholic, the fearful virgin, or the heterosexual whose promiscuity is equally compulsive however more conventional it may be in expression. In special situations, of course, homosexual behavior may be as normal a response to deprivation as masturbation, which once was regarded with an equally irrational horror.

If, nevertheless, we are to regard homosexuality as a personality problem, which is both a source and a manifestation of emotional disturbance, we should also be aware of how intimately the homosexual's distress, when it is felt as distress, derives from the expectation of adverse social reaction. The refusal of society to deal with homosexuality in a mature and positive way has tended to emphasize the sordid aspects of homosexual behavior. Because of this social situation, to the practicing psychotherapist at least, the ''cure'' of homosexuality by psychoanalytic methods alone seems an unrealistic goal. As Rieff says, ''Psychoanalysis does not cure; it merely reconciles.'' Self-acceptance and a more secure possession of his identity as an individual are of greater significance to the homosexual patient than conversion to what is called *sexual normality*. Better less neurotic, in other words, than merely more heterosexual.

The psychotherapist and the observant sociologist are alert both to the increasing awareness, and rising prevalence, of male homosexuality in contemporary America. (Because of a widespread surplus of females in the Western world, and because certain kinds of behavior are conventionally permissible for women but arouse suspicion when they are shown by men, homosexuality among women has evoked much less attention.) In metropolitan areas, at least—of course, nonconformists of all sorts tend to drift toward the shelter of metropolitan anonymity and the snug harbors of metropolitan fellowship—most people are familiar with, and many are intrigued by, homosexuality. Greater knowledge about sexual and psychological development, greater curiosity about human behavior in general, and greater sexual permissiveness have all contributed to this increased awareness of homosexuality.

No longer do plays on homosexual themes risk being closed by the police. Even films (especially if they are European) can approach the homosexual as a human being rather than as a dark mystery. Novelists more current than Gide and Proust find the homosexual interesting as a subject, but rarely do they produce anything approaching literature as a result, although Gore Vidal's *The City and the Pillar* has much to offer to the sensitive reader. Interestingly, as far as sales are a measure of acceptability, the lesbian heroine is more attractive to readers than the homosexual hero. For some women, perhaps, the lesbian is to be envied because she has found someone other than a man to serve her; to some heterosexual men the lesbian is peculiarly intriguing because she presents the ultimate challenge to male pride (or perhaps the ultimate threat, since she has no use for his most precious possession). And if the homosexual man is hostile to women, he may well enjoy seeing them, as lesbians, making each other unhappy enough to be good subjects for novels.

Thus far we have discussed the kind of awareness of homosexuality that has some claim to literacy, if not high artistic achievement. But even the columns of cheap magazines proffer advertisements for material that pretends to provide information and purvey salacity about homosexuals—and keeps neither promise.

Certainly we talk more about homosexuality than we used to, but are there proportionately more homosexuals? One cannot help thinking of nineteenth-century America with its mining camps where even squaws were scarce, its whalers often years out of sight of land, its remote army posts—not always provided with the "laundresses" who drew rations in George Washington's army; and its ranges where the only females belonged to other species. Statistics are not available for comparison, of course, but many social scientists maintain that the incidence of homosexuality has indeed increased.

This presumed increase of homosexuality is most usefully understood in the context of social crisis and of family disintegration, which is part of the critical transition that contemporary society is experiencing. Society in America, always fluid, has become all but amorphous, even while individuals are increasingly aware of, and anxious about, status. Competitiveness sharpens, and deep personal relationships become a source of competitive disadvantage. The person with ties, whether to places or people, is less prepared to compete, less able to move and to "fit in." Sexual as well as social roles are harder to learn in such a society and are perhaps less useful when they are learned; behavior patterns that are too thoroughly established may well make people less effectively mobile.

Human relations, as a result, have tended to become superficial and brief. Amid the general breakdown in communication between people, amid the deepening sense of alienation, sexuality, too, has taken on the aspects of a competition: sexual activity has become all but a rival of money as a measure for estimating and evaluating human beings. Many a person shows an almost compulsive desire to display his sexual appetites. What once was cherished in privacy now must be displayed to all the world. Men have always bragged of their success with women, if literature is a reliable witness; and women have counted their conquests. But both have usually kept their sexual needs to themselves; if they flaunted and even fostered unhappy love, it was to show constancy and a capacity for suffering, not to exhibit neuroses.

Our sexual mores *have* loosened, but fear and hatred of sex have not necessarily diminished. Indeed, sexual activity sometimes seems a screen against the dangers inherent in all human relationships. Often, giving another person affection seems a risk greater than the contemporary American is willing to take. For one man to give a member of his own sex and age any physical sign of affection is tabooed. And, as we shall see, some of the means that parents and educators seem to be using to prevent what they consider dangerously close relationships among adolescent boys actually promote durable homosexuality later on.

Because so many human relationships have become thin, casually hail-fellow-well-met instead of what is felt as perilously intimate, deviation is evident in aspects of sexual behavior that are not usually considered perverse. This is particularly true of divorce, which has become an increasingly common experience (the rising proportion of Roman Catholics in America notwithstanding). Less and less can a child take it for a matter of course that he will spend his early years with the same people in the role of parents. The middle-class family that once put down roots after a move or two often now regards moving as part of its way of life. A child may accept physical uprooting easily enough without psychological injury, provided that his parents are sufficiently close to give the child's life a core of stability. This was quite evident during the war years when children whose families were emotionally intact, who had at least one parent to rely on, proved surprisingly well able to withstand hardship and disruption. But when father, mother, brother, sister, all seem as easy to trade in as the car, the child finds it extremely difficult to establish an identity, to know who he is or what.

The family seems to be disintegrating. Gone are the days when children know what to expect from their parents and vice versa. Even among brothers and sisters, competitiveness has increased; sibling rivalry has become more pronounced; the possibility for normal development has diminished. This is the setting, within the larger instability of a constantly changing technological society poised on the edge of war, that provides the background for understanding the increase of male homosexuality in the United States.

For the growing boy—and it is his problems that concern us here—the contemporary family provides neither refuge nor models. All through history man and woman have played sharply defined roles in their societies. During this half-century, these roles have changed considerably in our Western world. And, we should remember, existence as man or woman is not dependent on the mere biological fact of having male or female sex organs. In our world existence has been increasingly linked to the role that society assigns. The German sociologist Helmut Schelsky has pointed out that the role man has to play in contemporary society has become ever more difficult, and Schelsky wonders whether the structure of our modern society is itself not responsible for the difficulties that heterosexual relationships have encountered in that society. Today, Schelsky points out, men are caught in so many relationships and obligations that they are more concerned with adjusting themselves to the general social pattern than with establishing themselves in the role of being a man. Not only is the contemporary societal pattern peculiarly complex, but most modern occupations can be performed by women as well as by men. The typical ''manly'' or masculine vocations are rapidly disappearing, at least from the list of honorable activities. As occupations, blacksmith and hunter have disappeared; farmer, miner, lumberjack, and fisherman now work as much with machines as with male brawn. Even the professional soldier, insofar as he holds a position of command, sits behind a desk or perhaps a computer. The day of the military leader on horseback is over. The most masculine figure of modern warfare drops bombs on women and children or, at best, on airplane carriers.

If masculine occupations are decreasingly important in a technological economy—and one largely oriented to finance and public relations rather than to production at that—the masculine role in the family has also changed. The father no longer has the support for his masculinity that he derived from being the authority figure he was in the nineteenth century. The difficulty a man encounters in establishing himself in the father role is reflected in the difficulty sons often experience in identifying with their fathers and thus learning to envision themselves in the role of men and fathers.

As the father's place in the home, and particularly in the American home, has changed, so has that of the mother. Women have assumed a new place in society. Middle-class women now help support their families almost as a matter of course. Women not only do hard work—that has always been part of their lives in the home and outside—they hold well-paying and even reasonably well-regarded jobs. Since American women have long enjoyed a scarcity value they did not have in modern Europe (until quite lately men have outnumbered women in most sections of the United States), they have not troubled to disguise their new position as their European counterparts did. The American woman appears unfeminine, that is, assertive rather than subtly manipulative. But well before the middle-class American woman had taken a place in business and the professions, her husband had given her basic command of her home and children so that he might be free to concentrate on making money.

The confusion of roles in the American family is not entirely new, then, but it has been intensified by the swiftness with which society is changing. In our American society, tradition and custom can play only a minor part. The pattern of stability, which the father no longer reliably supplies to the family, has increasingly become the function of the mother. Even in her possessiveness, the mother quite often represents the only remnant of the support that society once gave the person. Thus, the mother has acquired an increasingly important place. If she is of the castrating type, she can emasculate her son; at best, she can readily inspire him with fear and distrust of all women.

In the meantime, the boy turns to his contemporaries for models of masculinity. But they, too, have been brought up by mothers more or less like his own and by fathers uncertain of their maleness. The boy becomes at once competitive and self-doubting. So insecure are many American youths about their basic masculinity that we see an almost pathological emphasis on muscular development or athletic ability. Often, and again with parental encouragement, as a further spur to the development of a pseudomasculinity in boys who get so little real help in identifying themselves as males, we see parents all but frantically insistent that their children begin adult social life—including "dates"—when they are only ten and eleven. Where the middle-class boy once passed his teens in a kind of intimate camaraderie with his friends, today he must be socially successful with girls or be considered "sissified." A youth unprepared to meet such emotional responsibilities may well seek refuge from girls and their demands and find reassurance in being accepted homosexually.

With fathers unable to supply adequate patterns of masculinity, mothers possessive to the verge of being castrating, girls of his own age group forthrightly demanding, and society pressing him for professional and business success, the modern man may well seem pushed into a flight from masculinity. Abram Kardiner reports patients as saying that homosexual partners were once hard to find; now such companions are almost too available. Many contemporary young men see a relationship with a woman—especially if that relationship has any emotional depth—as taking on all the difficulties that acceptance of the masculine role implies and imposes.

The number of heterosexuals who have incidental homosexual experiences gives further evidence of the contemporary withdrawal from masculinity. Many overt homosexuals have had experience with "straight guys" who find a curious, impersonal kind of relief in such encounters, free as they are of genuine involvement. Such desire for noninvolvement is itself part of the pathos of alienation. Such incidental homosexuality, as it may be called, illustrates the crisis that all too many males experience in our society. The youth is caught between what others expect of him and what he does not desire for himself. He has few chances for physical adventure or even intense and clearly worthwhile physical activity. Chances for a real comradeship have diminished, though the desire continues, as is distortedly illustrated by the fighting gangs of our great cities. The United States has never had youth movements of the kind known in Europe. The male in our society is essentially a lonely being, deprived of any real goal except that of acquiring the skills needed to make money enough to "settle down" into an existence that he accepts rather than chooses.

In this situation, where conformity and early marriage are prescribed although our sexual mores have lost much of their strictness, it is not surprising to find an increasing number of men accepting homosexuality as a way out. Yet homosexuality can scarcely be considered a way of life. Indeed, the man who accepts that notion gives sexual "acting out" so important a place in his existence that he may cease to function as an effective person.

The homosexual who finds himself troubled by the effect of such obsessive behavior may well go into psychotherapy to be relieved of his neurotic concentration on sex rather than to change the direction of his sexual objective. Successful therapy does not remove the initial cause of homosexuality in such cases. Often, it cannot even explain that cause.

An effort to give such an explanation is the sociologist's responsibility. He is, or should be, concerned with inquiry into the relationship between the rise in male homosexuality and the decline of the authoritarian father.

The human being is increasingly depersonalized in our world. He is alienated from himself and others. Man is alone in ways he never has experienced before.

If we look at homosexuality in our age, we are struck by its relationships to the individual's need to settle for second-best and yet to question the settlement he has not fully accepted. As the German social psychiatrist Hans Giese points out, contemporary homosexuality must be studied in a context other than that of mere sexual pathology. It is part of a larger, an existential problem. The homosexual, like every other person, must be aware of his behavior and of his attitudes toward that behavior; he must learn to be concerned less with the origin of his problem and more with how he deals with that problem. Does he accept himself for what he is and go on to experience more complete ''being in the world'' or does he compulsively project his own inclinations onto others? Can he, in other words, be a person first and homosexual second?

To be sure, at least some segments of society are moving into a more mature, a less terrified attitude toward homosexuality, even in this open society where ruling groups continuously, though perhaps unconsciously, experience some kind of threat from those pressing upward. In such a society, competition for economic position may be felt as endangering the possession of masculinity; if male members of the energetic lower-class group are felt sexually attractive as well, the citadel of maleness truly stands besieged.

Nevertheless, homosexuality is increasingly being taken for granted as a social phenomenon, not an unmentionable sin. Even the relationship between its increase and the high cost of metropolitan living can be seen. The need for friendship in the isolation of a large city, the passing of the old-fashioned boardinghouse, and the consequent practicality of sharing an apartment may well have contributed to the development of intimacy between men who, even in the recent past, would never have dreamed of becoming sexually involved with another man. Again, although the middle-class woman may be more available sexually than she was half a century ago, her independent earning power makes her more difficult to provide for as a nonworking wife and mother and threateningly competitive if she does hold a job. Thus, the opportunity for developing homosexual behavior patterns are more frequent, and the choice of these patterns becomes more feasible in the rootless mobility of contemporary society.

If we see increasing homosexuality as a characteristic of the dissolution of a society, we can classify homosexuals into three groups, each showing a distinctive psychological and sociological picture. First, let us look at the covert homosexual. Unlike the latent homosexual, who neither has experience nor admits his desire for sexual contact with other men, the covert homosexual seeks sporadic experience but refuses to admit his homosexuality, even to himself. He may even have committed himself to marriage and family life. Within himself, therefore, he experiences conflict between the pattern of life he has chosen and the desire for homosexual experience. But it is not only the married man who may be a covert homosexual; a man may be unmarried and even heterosexually promiscuous and yet engage in a pattern of behavior, of relationship with other men, which he refuses to admit as genuine homosexuality.

It is the covert homosexual whose sexual experience is most sordid because it is apt to occur in rest rooms, subway stations, and the other shoddy corners that big cities provide. Such experiences can become peculiarly terrifying, colored with the shadow of nightmare, even more because the compulsive acting out may represent an inability to choose between homosexuality and heterosexuality. Homosexual encounters are even denied, as it were, forced into forgetfulness. It is these people who are most apt to stress the masculine ideal. To admit that one is masculinely defective would admit failure to live up to the ideal and hence bring the individual to realize that he is blocking off part of his personality.

Overt homosexuals do not, as a rule, block off this aspect of themselves. They know what they are, although they may have severe identity problems in other areas of their lives. Some overt homosexuals think of themselves as a minority group, as much entitled to its place in our pluralistic society as any other. Generally, this type of homosexual commits himself to a certain cultural attitude and to living within his minority, as it were. He is often slightly, or even strongly, effeminate. He cultivates a snobbery of his own, a "wit," an interest—often superficial—in the arts. He lives fast and moves often; today he is in New York, tomorrow in California. He cherishes his youth and has an all but pathological fear of aging. Settling down is abhorrent, the nonhomosexual world unbearably dull. Often he associates with only two types of women, lesbians and women who are not lesbian, but are frigid, and hence find themselves most comfortable with men in whom they can detect no threat of desire for themselves. This group of homosexuals often lacks stability; with some exceptions, its members do not possess the self-discipline necessary for successful work. Often, when they reach their forties, these people realize that middle age, however desperately fought off, cannot be delayed indefinitely. It is usually at this period in their lives that such overt homosexuals—aspirants to perpetual adolescence we might call them—come face to face with the pieces of their shattered lives and try, often vainly, to build mature existences out of the pieces.

The second variety of overt homosexual does not typecast himself. He lives outside the homosexual world, for the most part, engages in more conventional, that is, nonartistic, kinds of work and accepts more of the responsibilities of maturity. Promiscuity is less essential to his happiness than to that of members of the first group. Often he maintains stable personal relationships. Although he makes little effort to conceal his homosexuality, he does not turn homosexuality into a way of life. He, too, may suffer from guilt. He, too, fears age and the loss of sexual attractiveness. In contrast to the rebellious, flaunting type of homosexual, however, the man in this second group is willing to recognize the world as it is and to try to function within it. If he stands up to himself successfully, he can eradicate his fear of the heterosexual world and maintain an existential awareness that he himself can master his situation. His life is not easy, of course, but it is more likely to be productive and satisfying than the irresponsible life cultivated by the first group of homosexuals.

Ironically, the radical social mobility of the United States, the alienation and loneliness of the contemporary life, the disorganization of the family—all the basic causes for the rise of homosexuality in present-day America—also make it easier for the homosexual to function. In a rigidly structured society where family ties are tight and permanent, the homosexual is visibly outside the social fabric (unless he settles for some traditional form of celibacy, which imposes other problems). In a society as fluid as ours, the very confusion of roles makes it simpler to wear a succession of social masks without being truly identified with any. This may be basically detrimental, but for the nonconformist it has some convenient aspects, too. Thus, the sober white-collar worker, for example, can shut his office door and head for a homosexual bar or restaurant where he may be recognized as part of the culture and still maintain some anonymity as an individual. Whether these are desirable places to seek sexual partners is questionable, of course, but they are less legally perilous than parks or streets and certainly more appealing than rest rooms. The heterosexual man, incidentally, often complains that in our great cities men have real difficulty in meeting suitable women.

The increase in male homosexuality must be seen in the light of the general increase of social deviation in our world. Alongside an almost compulsive conformity, there is a widespread repudiation of what society considers "normal" or "acceptable." The beats, the juvenile delinquents, the rebellious young protesting, often in noisy silence, what Paul Goodman calls *growing up absurd* and Edgar Friedenberg *vanishing adolescence,* the confusion of roles and the absence of goals and expectations—all these have led some young people to question all current moral values and standards of behavior. This crumbling of barriers has brought sex deviation into focus and consequently has affected sexual behavior among youths and young women, too.

Coupled with the general instability and both the awareness and *increase* of neurotic behavior in our society, we see how the problem of achieving identity that besets man in an organizational society has also affected his sexual behavior. When pressured severely, the individual is apt to turn to unconventional channels of sexual expression. He is less apt to question the motives for his behavior than to see it simply as experience, which is part of his unique existence. Homosexuality is only part of the frequently tragic search for real experience in a world that, to many people, seems to have been stripped of all that once supported their humanity from outside. Man stands alone now; class, rank, family, even the fundamental sex role no longer props him up. He must choose the very basis of his existence. Life as a homosexual is one of the turnings he can take. It is a road an increasing number of men are following. The sociologist is less concerned that they do take this road than in knowing what in our society encourages them to do so. The psychoanalyst continues to have a scholar's interest in what in the patient's past made him susceptible to society's encouragement to take the homosexual way, but as a therapist, he is concerned that the homosexual patient learn to recognize and deal with all the determinants of his present human existence.

II

It is interesting to note that recent studies of homosexuality have moved away from traditional Freudian psychoanalytic explanations. The work of Irving Bieber [1] is an example of the traditional approach. The central finding of his study of a highly selected group of male homosexuals was emphasis on the proportion of subjects whose mothers could be described as close-binding and intimate and whose fathers were detached and hostile. These mothers, it is argued, selected this male child to protect and, inadvertently, to seduce. In the process of child rearing, the boy's sexual interest was both elicited and then blocked by punishing its behavioral manifestations. As a result of the mother's special ties to the child, the father is further alienated from familial interaction, becomes more hostile to his son, and fails to offer him any reason for becoming attached to the traditional male role.

The rather engaging and persuasive character of this theory is not without flaws. It assumes, for example, that there is a necessary relationship between the development of masculinity (or femininity) and the sexual behavior pattern of heterosexuality and homosexuality. It assumes, too, that homosexuals play sexual roles that are explicitly modeled upon heterosexual conduct and that these sex roles are well-defined and widespread. This sexual object choice is equated with masculine and feminine sexuality.

Equating these dimensions of sexuality constitutes a confusion based on two complementary errors: The source of error first lies in the characterization of behavior: even the physical sexual activities of the homosexual are often distinguished as passive (to be read, feminine) or active (to be read, masculine); and these physical activities are treated as direct homologues of the whole complex issue of masculinity and femininity. The second source of confusion lies in the two situations where homosexuality can be most easily observed. One is the prison. There homosexuality does tend to model itself rather closely on patterns of heterosexuality in the outside community. Yet in prison both the source and the character of behavior are in the service of different ends. The second situation is that of flaunted homosexuality, characterized by the blatant caricature of female gesture, which has become stereotypic homosexuality. Such heterosexuals' images of the nature of homosexuality may well affect the behavior of homosexuals. Nevertheless, the existence and even the real influence of stereotypes does not mean that they play a role in the etiology of the behavior that those stereotypes describe and explain.

Another major question raised by etiological theories of homosexuality based on family structure is the difficulty inherent in all theories based on data derived from individuals' reports of childhood memories. Such theories rely on hearsay not only about the reporter himself, but about his parents.

HOMOSEXUALITY: A
CONTEMPORARY VIEW

We live in a post-Freudian world. The vocabulary of even the psychologically illiterate is heavy with terms like *repression, inhibition, the Oedipus complex,* and *castration fears.* The language of psychoanalysis permeates American culture as a result of a process that might be called the *democratization* of professional knowledge about mental illness and of the aspiration toward mental health. One lesson of existentialism is that our biographies are not stable stories. A person's life as he perceives it is subject to revision, elision, and other forms of editing based on one's place in the life cycle, his audience, and his current mask. Indeed, for many persons the past rehearsed and the real past are so intermingled that only the present really exists. Recent research in child-rearing practices suggests that two years after the major events of child-rearing—weaning and toilet training—mothers no longer really remember their previous conduct and hence tend to sound a good deal like Dr. Spock. (It is of course important to remember that the past is not always edited to produce a better image in the conventional sense. Patients in psychotherapy often work very hard to bring out more and more self-denigrating material to assure the therapist that they really are working hard and searching for their real motives.)

From a sociological point of view, the original causes of homosexuality may not even be very important for understanding the patterns of homosexual behavior observed in a given society. Much as the medical student who comes to medicine for many reasons, and for whom the homogenous character of professional behavior arises from the experiences of medical school rather than from the root causes of his choice of occupation, so the patterns of adult homosexuality grow out of the social structures and values that surround the homosexual person after he becomes, or conceives of himself as, homosexual rather than upon the root causes of his choice of sexual object.

I suggest that the homosexual's sexual object has come to dominate our imagery of the homosexual person. Hence, this aspect of his total life experience appears to determine all his concerns and activities. Nonhomosexuals seem concerned only with the purely sexual aspect of the homosexual's life. Such a concentration of concern would be rejected by students interested in the heterosexual. The mere presence of sexual deviation seems to give the sexual content of life an overwhelming significance. Thus, although homosexuals vary profoundly in the degree to which their homosexual commitment becomes the organizing principle of their lives, that commitment is seen as determining the rest. Consequently, in dealing with homosexuals, whether in theory or in therapy, students tend to forget that the homosexual individual's problems are the problems of a person, and are even likely to be explained by the originating circumstances rather than by the consequences of establishing the commitment itself.

Even with the relatively recent shift in the normative framework available for considering homosexuality—that is, from a rhetoric of sin to a rhetoric of mental health—the preponderance of the sexual factor is evident. The change may have major significance in the legal and social treatment of homosexuals. Nevertheless, the mental health rhetoric seems to go as wide of the mark as the rhetoric of sin in helping us understand homosexuality. One advance has been made, of course. Whether writers use one rhetoric or the other, they tend to replace the concept of optimum behavior with a discussion of the psychological characteristics necessary for a person somehow to survive within specific social systems and social situations.

Obviously, the satisfaction of a homosexual commitment makes social adjustment more difficult than it might be for people who accept the heterosexual way of life. What is important to understand, however, is that consequences of these sexual practices are not necessarily direct functions of the nature of such practices. It is necessary to move away from an obsessive concern with the sexuality of the individual and attempt to see the homosexual more personally, in terms of the broader attachments that he must make in order to live in the world around him. Like heterosexual people, homosexuals must come to terms with the problems attendant upon living in society: the homosexual, too, must find a place to work; he must learn to live with, or without, his family;

he must be involved or apathetic in political life; he must find a group of friends to talk to and live with; he must fill his leisure time usefully or frivolously. Like everyone in the culture, the homosexual must cope with all the problems, common and uncommon, of impulse control and personal gratification; he, too, must socialize his sexual interests in some fashion if he intends to live at relative peace in the society.

There is a seldom-noticed diversity to be found in the life cycle of the homosexual, both in terms of solving general human problems and in terms of the particular characteristics of the life cycle itself. Not only are there as many ways of being homosexual as there are of being heterosexual, but the individual homosexual, in the course of his everyday life, encounters as many choices and as many crises as the heterosexual. It is much too easy to allow the label, once applied, to suggest that the complexities of role transition and identity crises are easily attributable to, or are a crucial exemplification of, some previously existing etiological defect.

Among the varieties of sexuality, fetishism ranks high in occurrence and intensity. Traditional sexologists like Hirschfeld and Krafft-Ebing cited considerable clinical material on fetishism; one of Freud's early pupils, Wilhelm Stekel, described an interesting case of apron fetishism in his *Sexual Aberrations* where he described fetishism as ''a curious combination of synthesis and antithesis.'' [1] Traditional psychoanalysts, of course, believe with Freud that the fetish is a penis-substitute. [2]

Analysts of this school think that the fetishist begins to experience his desires even at a very early age. Karl Abraham, another of Freud's early pupils, stresses this point in his classic paper on foot and corset fetishism. [3] Another pioneer of the Freudian school, Sandor Lorand, illustrates this point in a remarkable study of a four-year-old boy who exhibits characteristically fetishistic behavior. Lorand moves beyond the consensus of psychoanalytic opinion on fetishism when he declares: ''Fetishism saves the individual from becoming homosexual but saves him, at the same time, from becoming normal, which would bring the danger of castration.'' [4]

Post- and neo-Freudian analysts have tended to move away from the orthodox interpretation of fetishism. Social psychologist Ernest Becker describes what may be called fetishism in persons who are relatively conventional in sexual behavior: ''If fetishism, by definition, connotes

FETISHISM:
HETEROSEXUAL AND
HOMOSEXUAL

the merger of poverty and ingenuity, we also know that none of us is exempt from the 'disease.' We are all relatively poor and ingenious. This is what permits us to handle, with full devotion and finely tuned capability, a very definite area of the object world. Without routine compulsiveness, we would all literally fade away; we would be able to marshal no ego at all. The more our powers are limited, and the more some special commitment is wanted, the more we become alert to fetishistic cues to action. . . . Thus we are all more or less prone to fetishistic definitions in our sex life when we show a preference for a particular portion of our partner's body.''

Becker then distinguishes *normal* from *abnormal* fetishism. Fetishists, as Becker sees it, are persons more severely limited in sexual behavior than ordinary people rather than as persons who are basically different in their sexuality. People so limited must attach themselves to ''some perceptual detail,'' from which they derive their reason for being drawn to sexual feeling.[5]

Clinical treatment of the fetishist continues to be a demanding task. Even the current literature offers few instances where fetishists have been helped to surmount their preoccupations and achieve a more conventional form of expression for their sexual impulses. The following case of heterosexual fetishism is cited from recent clinical literature as an example of successful use of existential techniques in treating a fetishist.

Medard Boss here is dealing with K. S., the oldest child of prosperous and ill-assorted parents. K's father was a quiet, remote person whose family had apparently disliked reality, but not sufficiently to take refuge in a mental hospital. His mother, beyond bearing five children, had shown more concern with society than her home and left husband, household, and children to servants. Mrs. S. showed disgust at her children's physical needs, gave them no affection—indeed, rejected them rather thoroughly. K., as the oldest, seems to have drawn most hostility from her and to have been completely unprotected by his father, who allowed the mother to get the boy out of the way, sending him to a distant boarding school. There the boy was so unhappy that he withdrew into a fantasy world, a withdrawal that did not prevent schoolmates and, later, acquaintances from drawing him "into calamitous adventures."

As a youngster, K. S. had enjoyed looking at small girls and had even been ready to fondle them impulsively. Unhappiness at home and at school put an end to this. When sexuality reawakened in the adolescent, K. S. was attracted not to women but to the leather or fur wraps they happened to wear. The attraction spread from coats and capes to gloves and shoes, women's riding boots, particularly, from which "a strange halo," a magic force seemed to radiate. The god of love himself seemed to live in these objects and emerge from them to take possession of K. S.

Real female skin seemed revolting. Breasts and female genitalia were repulsive and roused intense feelings of guilt. A woman's bare foot was lifeless; that same foot in a shoe carried her into a sphere "where superhuman and subhuman" blended into something marvelous. Then, and then only, could K. S. feel true sexual desire and exert full potency.

Nevertheless, K. S. did fall in love and marry. His fiancée resembled his mother, a fact he did not notice, and seemed to share his anticipations of a mythologically (K. S. became a classical philologist) happiness in marriage. She could not understand, however, his "holy ceremony of love," which required her to put on furs or bearskin gloves before the love act, or his total impotence without resort to his fetishes.

K. S. found that his wife could not come into his fantasy world, and her failure made even his necessary fetishes lose their magic. Without them, he was impotent. With them, he knew his wife's revulsion.

Medard Boss then goes on to describe this patient's problem:

Daseinanalysis, or existential analysis, demands that we analyze the essential manifestations of life in its own formulations. If we add neither facts nor theoretic constructions to K. S.'s history of life and love, as it was expressed in his psychoanalysis, we must state that only once in his life had his heart been open and without barriers toward the female world, and this had been long ago, when he, at the age of five or six, had embraced and kissed strange little girls affectionately and wholeheartedly in the streets. Thereafter K. S.'s world narrowed, and he found himself stubbornly withdrawn into a dreary loneliness without comfort. Essentially, it was his mother who had failed in her maternal task of serving as a useful model and in constructing a bridge to future sympathetic love communication in the world of human relationship. Instead, she irrevocably locked the gate into the world, to the mode of existence of love, through her coldness, rigidity, and confining prudery toward all physical functions. Therefore, the whole world became cold and alien to him forever.

In his dreams his mother's corpse appeared amidst sunny land-scapes. Even in his sleep she spoiled his love for the natural world. His mother's unusual prudery ruined K. S.'s vital relationship to the bodily aspect of human existence. His own body had become an estranged tool even for motion and action, and it was inconceivable for him to regard bodies, especially women's bodies, as something lovable or attractive. A naked female body part remained to him ''a piece of meat in a butcher shop'' or it even conveyed to him ''suspicion, disgust and horror.'' This suspicion grew to threatening anxiety in dreams. He found himself amidst rotting women's corpses permeated with worms and bugs. The vermin aimed especially at his spirituality. Once in a dream he made the greatest effort to finish the manuscript of some scientific work. However, each finished page was magically sucked into and devoured by worms in a deep yawning abyss at his feet. Just like the fetishist of Von Gebsattel,* K. S. had numerous non-fetishistic incest dreams about his mother, in which he actually slept with his mother and which left him with the strongest sexual excitement. Interestingly enough, he never saw fetishes in his dreams.

One cannot doubt the presence and significance of K. S.'s incest and

* German sexologist and psychoanalyst.

castration complexes, evidently manifested in such stubbornly repeated dreams, and his strong emotional reactions to them, even though one disregards the great actual external resemblance between his mother and his wife. We know that psychoanalysis deserves the credit for having directed our attention toward these important and ubiquitous complexes. It is, however, our own position that neither can we derive the incest or castration fear from historical grounds (whether their roots are understood sociologically or through hereditary biology,[6] as psychoanalytic theory stated in its positivistic philosophy), nor can we accept Oedipus complex or castration fear as factual causes of all neurotic anxiety and repressions.

In the method of Daseinanalysis, anxiety signifies a basic mode-of-being-here (in the world): It is the special mode of existing in which the human being experiences complete worldly isolation and the menace of the absolute not-existing, the "nothing" (Heidegger). In our opinion, incest, Oedipus complex, and castration fear indicate only inroads and apertures where anxiety—inherent in all existence—may break into one's world. Accordingly we regard both incest taboo and castration fear only as concrete realizations of the essential, basic arch-anxiety (primal anxiety) innate to all isolated, individual forms of human existence. In the basic anxiety itself human existence is afraid of, as well as anxious about, its "being-in-the-world" (Heidegger). Actually, the incest taboo conceals the commandment that human, earthly life should exist in myriads of separated individual particles . . . only super-worldly gods and kings at the dawn of history were granted the right of mother or sister incest, because they alone were not asked to live an earth-bound, split-up existence. . . . Mortals, however, in mythologies, psychoses, dreams, and fantasies encounter the disastrous punishment of castration for violating the incest taboo.[7]

The fear of castration on the other hand makes transparent the existential anxiety about the continuity of human existence in the mode of earthly confined individuals.[8]

Before K. S.'s existential anxiety could have been experienced by

FETISHISM: HETEROSEXUAL AND HOMOSEXUAL

him in its concrete manifestations as the fears of the Oedipus and castration complexes, it had overshadowed his life in a vague and unassailable way. We find such anxiety in its greatest form with psychotics and primitives.[9] K. S. used to say: "I always feel hemmed in and isolated as if under an anxiety-lid. This anxiety-lid permanently presses on my heart." Anxiety, being the most characteristic "fundamental disposition of human existence" (Heidegger), is the most important barrier of the worldly isolated mode of existence, with its limits in time and space and limitations through narrow purposes. Thus, anxiety, significant as a barrier, represents the essential anthropologic counter pole of love. It covers up completely the fullness, broadness, depth, rootedness, infinity, and eternity of existence that are inherent experiences of the mode of being in love.

In interpreting the life history of K. S. we understand that especially the physical-sensuous spheres of his existence could be experienced by him only in the worldly finite and isolated way of existing with its anxiety and other earthly narrowness. These regions, therefore, could be looked at but with "hostile suspicion, disgust, horror, and guilt feelings."

K. S.'s heavy "anxiety-lid" could not even be lifted by the sensuous and instinct-driven onset of puberty. This "anxiety-lid" had hardened under the influence of the mother's lovelessness and her unnatural behavior toward all physical bodies and especially female ones. Therefore, even when K. S. had grown to manhood the female body did not carry the translucent and transparent quality leading to the entirety of loving experience. We must also remember that the closer the bodily region was anatomically or functionally situated to the female sex pole, the more this uncomfortable feeling was increased to actual fear and disgust.[10] He was unable to even think of the female genitals without experiencing real disgust and horror. The mere thought of these things seemed to him a sacrilege.

We can understand that K. S. proved to be perfectly impotent during normal sexual contact with his beloved, who was later his wife. Her body was caught in his inflexible world pattern and cornered by his walls of anxiety. He had to escape into the sphere of general fantasies and impersonal mythologies—into the high-flown spheres into which an irresistible power had drawn him in his dreams. Not only had K. S. been able to keep free the topmost spheres of his existence from impenetrable ''anxiety-lids and anxiety-walls,'' in spite of his impossible upbringing, he was also able to ''lower'' the region of perceptibility of love's pervasiveness in the ''genito-petal'' direction ''down'' into the most unbodily sex-remote and therefore anonymous trappings of a female body. This enabled him to include gloves, pieces of fur, and shoes into his ''love ceremony.'' They at least were given to him as ''vessels'' in which ''lust of love and deepest pleasure'' could be realized—could become concrete. However, all the other manifestations of human existence, which lay closer to the sex poles of the woman under these wraps, were increasingly covered, guarded, and fenced in through the worldly barriers of disgust, suspicion, and horror, which prevented the entrance of love into this existential figure whose name was K. S.

We believe that we can understand the meaning, the content, and the genetic conditioning of fetishism only on the basis of such a concept of the existential structure and its corresponding world scheme. The old association theory of Binet, which at first was also used by Freud, could not adequately justify the essence of fetishism. Alfred Binet's theory of perversion and especially of fetishism was traced back to more or less accidental connections of primary infantile sexual stimulation with the presence of any external object or sexually remote part of the body.[11] Actually, however, such factors of a life history cannot explain the real meaning of the specific fetishistic exclusiveness of such tying together. Instead, we have to evaluate such early sexual stimulation through isolated objects or body parts as primary expressions by and manifestations of the already preconditioned fetishistic existential structure of a specific child. Since a child's relationship to the mother represents the primary and most significant gate to the mode-of-being of love into existence, many analyses of fetishes actually indicate that their specific shaping is due to the mother's world at that time. However, this need not be so. In the case of K. S. we can exclude with certainty the fact that neither the mother nor any other person who had taken care of him had ever worn bearskin gloves. But bearskin or furs as such are of eminent physical-sensuous symbolic significance. The bearskin of K. S., then, is, as is the case with many other fetishists, the transmitter of the whole magic superindividual human-godly femininity which can pervade it, skipping the connection with the concrete human reality of mother-love.

Psychoanalysis soon recognized the insufficiency of the Binet association theory of perversions and had ascribed to the fetish "in a deeper level" the role of a "cover memory," meaning that the fetish always represented the unconscious repressed symbol of the motherly phallus. Castration shock has motivated the repression.[12] We, however, think that such interpretation is characteristic of the concretistic positivistic narrowing of the psychoanalytic theory, a narrowness that compresses the wholeness and fullness of the love experience into a mere organ. In interpreting female underwear as fetishes, this theorem forced Freud to the strained and most improbable construction of these garments (by virtue of their covering up female genitals), to suggest the presence of a maternal penis as well as the possibility of castration. This, Freud states, constitutes their fetishistic attraction.

Throughout the entire analysis, K. S. held on to the bearskin and the bearskin gloves as having decidedly feminine, nonphallic significance. The same was true with two other fetishists who used feminine underwear as their love objects. We also know of perverted people whose fetishes have phallic meaning. But in such cases the problem is not fetishism as such but a complicated homosexuality. We therefore could prove an impressive phallic meaning of the fetish only with men who themselves had realized too little of their own manliness in their real life. They had to dream of male fetishes, because one reaches out to other spheres for things one does not have oneself. To this kind of atrophic human personality, realizing so very little of all the possibilities of human existence, the phallic mother image then has to represent and substitute for everything that is missing within themselves, that is, for the entire male and female existential pattern.[13]

With the rejection of the interpretation of the fetish as a motherly phallus, we do not any longer have the seemingly plausible explanation that Freud gave for the extraordinary preponderance of fetishes among men. With women this variety of sexuality is, as we know, exceedingly rare.

We ask ourselves whether this peculiarity of fetishism may be derived from the fact that in the typical existential masculine pattern, the imaginary power plays a greater part than in the typically feminine pattern; and that a man perceives the world in a more universal spirit and conceives more abstract spiritual and perhaps phantastic connections and images, while female experiences of the world and love remain more bound to the concrete personal sphere. This could mean that men were still able to experience a certain existential and loving fullness transparent through the anonymous, peripheric, impersonal gestalt sector of a fetish though it is quite separated from the concrete body of a specific individual. Women who would reject love from the physical realm of the concrete partner to the same degree would react with total frigidity.

K. S.'s love experiences contradict in an even deeper sense the "anthropologic theory" (as originated by Von Gebsattel, who used the example of fetishism, and later developed by E. Straus and H. Kunz). Anthropologists, up to the present, always stated that every pervert acquired his sexual excitement basically from deforming factors, such as aggressive impulses, which in their perverted actions were directed against the love norm. The fetishists then derived their sexual excitement from the "fetishistic partitioning" or "division" of the whole love object.

The sexual excitement, however, does not stem from this narrowing of the love transparency. On the contrary, K. S. retained his ability to experience his sexuality only because the ''deformation,'' the ''anxiety-lid,'' had left open to him some peripheric sector of the female figure as the entrance gate to the mode-of-being of love into the world. What the ''anthropologic'' theory recognizes is only the pathologic ''darkening'' of the fetishistic world, yet it does not explain the essence of the fetishist's love. The mode of existence of love in itself is not disturbed, but in the narrowed world of the fetishist it can only express itself in the physical and sensual realm through the fetishistic periphery of the female existence.

In discussing fetishism one should not neglect its cultural aspects. Fashion and fads in clothing and ornaments often stimulate fetishistic tendencies in both men and women alike, although women, here as elsewhere, seem disinclined to turn to fetishism as a form of sexual expression.

Fetishism has played a significant role in homosexual behavior in recent years. Where a substantial number of homosexuals doubt their masculinity, they tend to overreact in display, thus seeking to establish their masculinity. The cult of leather, for example, is now recognized as an evident aspect of homosexual costuming.

There is an emphasis on the wearing of masculine clothes—leather pants, blue jeans, leather jackets, boots, all the trappings of the sportsman, and the characteristic ''work'' clothes of the man engaged in heavy manual labor. Of course there are strong links between such homosexual fetishism and the appearance and occurrence of sadomasochism in such homosexuals.[14]

Of course, as Becker remarked, contemporary society displays so much fetishism that many varieties may be regarded as normal. Certainly, the medallions, beads, and headbands of the ''hippie,'' ''yippie,'' ''crazy'' young are not essentially different from the old-school ties, the proper stickpins, the Homburg hats, which are essential to their conventional elders. And if some motorcycle gangs are known by their glass-studded leather belts, what about the huntsman's ''pink'' coat or the officer's swagger stick? One wonders whether today's increasing emphasis on the experience of sexuality—not as pleasure but as mark of silence—has not tended to bring to the surface the fetishistic tendencies that many people have so long been forced to conceal.

The implications of sadomasochism extend far beyond the clinical observations of the psychoanalyst. But certainly one of the most significant aspects of de Sade's *120 Days of Sodom* is the way in which it established the link between sexuality and the kind of behavior that has come to be labeled *sadism*. Certainly, de Sade did not intend to write a clinical study. It has been conjectured that much of the material in his novels represents the fantasies of a man shut away from human contact in prison. He had, as is well known, been jailed before the outbreak of the French Revolution for offenses against morality. Be that as it may, de Sade's work describes with amazing accuracy the sexual varieties that later would be discussed in the clinical studies of Hirschfeld and Krafft-Ebing.

It was left for Freud, however, to explore sexual aberration ''in depth.'' In writing about the roots of sadism, he states, ''The roots of active algolagnia, sadism, can be readily demonstrable in the normal individual. The sexuality of most men shows an admixture of *aggression,* of a propensity to subdue, the biological significance of which lies in the necessity for overcoming the resistance of the sexual object by actions other than mere courting. Sadism would then correspond to an aggressive component of the sexual impulse which has become independent

REFLECTIONS ON
DE SADE AND
SADOMASOCHISM

and exaggerated and has been brought to the foreground by displacement.''

As sadism makes the name of de Sade immortal, so ''masochism'' incorporates the name of Leopold Sacher-Masoch.[1] Like de Sade, Sacher-Masoch belonged to the upper class in a relatively decadent monarchy (Austria) and like him, Sacher-Masoch presented in fiction the kind of description of human sexual behavior that makes most clinical reporting seem pallid and uninformative. In his book *Venus in Furs,* Sacher-Masoch shows the connection between masochism and sexuality with peculiar clarity. In most of his work, incidentally, masochistic behavior is shown by the male protagonist who seeks out an aggressive, sadistic woman.[2]

Sadism and masochism are counterparts, the face and obverse of a coin, so to speak. Most psychoanalysts agree that masochism and sadism are not opposites, rather they are complementary counterparts in the actual dynamics of the personality. In the clinical evidence available, one seldom finds sadism unaccompanied by masochism.[3] Particularly, it has become clear that aggression plays as important a role in the structure of masochism as it does in sadism. As a matter of fact, Freud held the view that masochism is identical with primal sadism and is only increased by secondary masochism, a point he especially refers to in the opening section of his classic paper ''A Child Is Being Beaten.''

Once removed from sheer clinical aspects, sadism in society takes on different faces. There is indeed a great deal of sadism in the violence contemporary society experiences today. Although we always hear of sadism in the movies and cartoons, and although there are strong sexual overtones to some of the violence portrayed in movies and cartoons, it might be interesting to observe that we have not yet seen movies, or plays for that matter, that are sadistic in the classic literary and psychological sense of the term. Sadistic pornography, for example, from the days of de Sade down to *The Story of O* has always required *privacy.* Typically, the victim is abducted to a lonely castle, country house, or monastery from which rescue is impossible and where freedom is obtainable only ironically—through the complete submission to the will of the tormentor, who offers freedom from the heaviest obligation of ordinary life, the necessity of making choices and accepting their consequences.

"Must We Burn Sade?" begins in what appears to be a promising direction when Mme. de Beauvoir distinguishes herself from those who have so uncritically worshipped Sade and thus, she notes, have betrayed him. "The critics who make of Sade neither villain nor hero, but a man and a writer, can be counted," she asserts, "on the fingers of one hand. Thanks to them," she continues, "Sade has come back at last to earth." "It was not murder," she writes, "that fulfilled Sade's erotic nature: it was literature." Having made that most pertinent observation, she quite forgets it and having forgotten it, is lost. At another point: "The torturer disguised as lover delights to see the credulous lover swooning with voluptuousness and gratitude, mistake cruelty for tenderness." The obvious step, which simply requires the translation of "lover" into "reader" in relation to the torturer disguised as a writer, is not taken. "Torturer and victim," she points out, "recognize their fellowship in astonishment, esteem and even admiration" and elsewhere quotes Sade: "There is no keener pleasure for a libertine mind than to win proselytes." For this lady then, some reservations about his literary style and the coherence of his philosophy notwithstanding (for it must be clear that she has not given herself unreservedly: she would not betray him), Sade "deserves to be hailed as a great moralist." "His passionate self-absorption," she declares, "gave his life an exemplary character. . . . He made of his sexuality an ethic: he expressed that ethic in works of literature . . . . He went beyond the sensualism of age and transformed it into an ethic of authenticity." Even more curious is another judgment: "Sade's immense merit," she observes, "lies in his taking a stand against [those] abstractions and alienations which are merely flights from the truth about men. . . . He adhered only to the truths which were derived from the evidence of his own actual experience. . . . No one was more passionately attached to the concrete he." One must of course grant a certain kind of concreteness, but it is the kind that confines Geoffrey Gorer, English anthropologist, when he compares the *120 Days* with *The Castle*—quite the wrong kind in fact, unless one is willing to accept anatomical detail as a substitute for the imagination of the real, which in this context is incarnation. *"As for the type of incarnation that sadism would like to realize,"* Sartre had previously written, *"this is precisely what is called the Obscene."* "It was by means of his imagination," Mme. de Beauvoir argues, "that [Sade] escaped from space, time, prison, the police, the void of absence, opaque presences, the conflicts of existence, death, life and all contradictions."

Nowhere in her long and occasionally complicated essay does she come closer to a definition of the ailment and at no point is she more thoroughly perverse in her understanding. There is no little irony here, but unfortunately that irony serves neither Sade nor his admirer; rather, both are caught within it, neither apparently sensible to it. Having characterized Mme. de Beauvoir as victim and accomplice, one must now also regard her as virtually demonic in her relation to her subject. In the light of her praise, or what appears to be praise in the reflection of its own strange light, an appalling defect appears as an extraordinary gift, as it is by means of that gift that Sade makes his escape. (*"Sade himself . . . inhibited the tower of Freedom,"* Camus wrote, *"but in the Bastille."*) As though apprehensive that the precise dimensions of Sade's gift might elude us, Mme. de Beauvoir makes an inventory of those disasters and miseries from which his imagination saved him, and that inventory quite correctly includes life itself.[4]

The relevance of de Sade, and for that matter sadism, is reemphasized in our contemporary society, where today we are coping much more with the overt acts of sadomasochism. In an increasingly alienated society de Sade may also be the first to limn the modern consciousness, see the void around it. He wants to restore man to nature; he recognizes in man the dominion of instinctual forces. He perceives, with a rigor akin to Freudian determinism, the bizarre equivalences of mind and

REFLECTIONS ON DE SADE
SADOMASOCHISM

body, fantasy and flesh, in the pursuit of love. He has an intuition of the primal horde, the taboo against incest, the Oedipal drama we reenact continually with our fathers and mothers, brothers and sisters. He knows that dreams extend the meaning of our waking life and employs them in his stories accordingly. Above all, de Sade complicates for us, in a tragic and irrevocable way, the image of life-giving Eros by revealing the long shadow Thanatos casts upon it. He understands that violence is a condition of vitality, and that Nature revels in destruction; he brings the Enlightenment to an end. Yet he never loses the sense that love always lurks where death rules.

As Brigid Brophy has put it, "The unitive purpose of Eros is never wholly defeated, because in Sade's conception the torturer and victim tend towards what Simone de Beauvoir calls a genuine couple. Sade is aware that the torturer's real crime will not be simply to inflict pain but to seduce and corrupt the victim into being his accomplice and wanting pain to be inflicted. The relation comes close to being a game. . . ."

This is the game that may have become the apocalypse of our time.

# part 3 | SEXUALITY TODAY

I

There was a time when parents thought that silence about sexuality was the best way to deal with their children's questions—and problems—about sex. Until very recently, many parents found this attitude workable. But now they can no longer afford to stand by and let sexuality take care of itself. They simply must produce answers to the sexual questions of their children. The old tales about the begonias and the bees won't help parents deal with children nowadays; they are too sophisticated to accept that approach; they want to know about people, their parents, their peers, and above all, themselves.

Sexuality, as Paul Ricoeur remarks, has lost its ancient magic, its age-old sacred meaning. Sex has lost its mystery; there are no secrets anymore. With the vanishing of mysteries, sexuality has lost a great deal of the peculiar attraction of that which is unknown. Taboos have disappeared or are disappearing very rapidly. They no longer have any real place in our contemporary open society. In a society where relationships between parents and children have undergone fundamental changes, concepts of sexuality that might have worked fifty years ago are no longer relevant. In a society where old concepts are constantly being challenged, it is not surprising that established ideas on sexuality have now lost their impact.

CHILDREN, PARENTS, AND SEXUALITY

This statement, insistently, is not linked to the tiresome, worn-out concept "the conflict between the generations." No, it merely signifies that our world has reached the bottom of traditional sexuality.

In a society where parents have *ceased* to be parents in the traditional Victorian sense of the word, with father holding the purse strings and mother presiding over the household, children have changed accordingly. The disappearance of *innocent* childhood, along with the screening of ignorance about sex, and the greater assertiveness and independence of contemporary children have created a social climate in which nineteenth-century sexual secrecy no longer holds any attraction and its hitherto artificially created attractiveness about sexual information is no longer valid. The notion that sexuality is itself a strange and wonderful mystery may even seem ridiculous in the eyes of contemporary children and parents.*

This has little to do with sex education in the schools, which seems to be an issue at present, but it has much more to do with sexuality itself *coming of age*. Social scientists and educators alike still get caught in particular details of sexual behavior and inflate their importance out of proportion. That sex education for example, should still be an issue is all but inconceivable in a world where sexuality is on continuous and often overt display.

Discussion about sexuality has been vastly expanded. The pill, abortion, and premarital and extramarital intercourse are now freely talked about in mixed company and all kinds of circles, including that outdated institution the Church. It seems only a question of time when these problems will be of no importance even to those who are still excited

---

* This author maintains that children in traditional terms will eventually disappear. Indeed until the eighteenth century, childhood as we know it did not really exist. There were only small human beings and larger, wiser, more powerful ones. Today, the nineteenth-century borders between adults, adolescents, and children have been blurred. There are no definite distinctions between adults and children in their social interaction. The day of the respectful, deferential child is over.

about them. It has always seemed ironic that the pill, abortion, and premarital and extramarital sex are not problems to those who take the pill, engage in premarital and extramarital intercourse, or do get an abortion. Rather these activities are problems only to people not directly involved, people who, incidentally, seem far behind their times; they are, in effect, still debating the French Revolution while the third world war is just around the corner.

Since the universe itself has long since ceased to be mysterious, however wonderful it may appear, it seems rather silly to suppose that sexuality can or ought to be kept under wraps. No one can keep sexuality locked up. Even in the Middle Ages, when sexuality was considered evil evidence of the devil's power over men, love found its way. Yet that way was too often unhappy. If sexuality in the Middle Ages was a secret mystery, it was also a repression. [1] We can well be relieved that sexuality has broken the barriers of past restraints.

Today's children and today's parents must see sexuality as a part, not as a problem, of their existence. True, sexuality has been made a problem between parents and children. Why, for example, should parents not be frank about their *own* sexuality? * Why not relate to the children some of their own feelings and perhaps anxieties about their own sexuality? This may sound unorthodox, but orthodoxy in communicating sexuality to children has no very distinguished record of success. If contemporary parents and children discuss everything else with each other, there seems small reason for their failure to talk frankly about sexuality. Such sessions between parents and children need not develop into some variety of pseudo-group therapy; rather they should develop a more open, frank discussion of some of the questions children . . . and even parents might have. Doing this means bringing sexuality out of the privacy of the bedroom and into the wider *realm* of day-to-day living.

* So many children have been frightened and revolted by the secret bedroom scenes between their parents, and it subsequently has colored their attitudes toward their own sexuality.

Division between sexuality and the rest of life has been the source of the difficulties families find in discussing sexual problems. There has been a real failure to make sexuality part of the *whole* experience of life. I see no reason why parents should not discuss the various *taboos* of sexuality with their children. Think of the anguish and torture homosexual children and adolescents endure only because they cannot talk about their desires and their experience with their parents, the persons to whom they are or should be closest.

Why should parents be protected from the sexual problems of their children? Provided that parents can handle themselves, a full discussion of such topics can only benefit the homosexual child or adolescent. For then the young people are aware that someone *cares* and *knows*. Frankness also helps to maintain the relationship between parents and their homosexual children. Many homosexuals have long felt the wound of being unable to *share* that important part of their life with their parents.[2]

Parents should no more project their own desires and wishes about the sexuality of their children than they should consider their children the objects through which they realize their own vocational ambitions. When parents recognize that their children have their own *sexual* lifestyle, they will be able to establish much healthier and friendlier relationships with them.

*Sexuality* must be recognized as a personal experience, *not* as a *prescribed* or preordained life experience. Paul Ricoeur has written on the *enigma* of sexuality.[3] For each person, sexuality is something of a puzzle, or better, a revelation. Sexuality is at the same time a discovery and a surprise to those who are beginning to explore that aspect of themselves. For all our factual knowledge and psychological insight, sexuality should continue to retain an aspect of surprise, of adventure. The clinical picture of sexuality, and parents should realize this, is not a complete portrait of sexual experience. Ignorance about sex is certainly not to be recommended, but the experience of sexuality, like the *experience* of all life, remains something of an enigma to everyone.

Questions about what parents should tell their children about sexuality will become more and more meaningless. Children will find out anyway. They always have. What is important is that parents transmit to their children an appreciation of the *dignity* of *all* sexual experiences. By clinging to the taboos and prejudices of the past, parents transmit to their children nothing beyond the distortions of sexuality, and these distortions will eventually hamper (or sometimes even cripple) their children's sexual development.

Parents who are afraid of talking freely and honestly about the sexual side of life better seek counsel for themselves. They certainly are not equipped to guide and enlighten their children about sexuality. And children should learn about *all* aspects of sexuality. The varieties of sexuality should no more be kept from them than the varieties of religious expression. It all is part of life itself, which children should be prepared to experience, in its fullness. Certainly ignorance of what are called the deviant aspects of sexuality may provoke the insecurities and anxieties that so often beset people who are ridden by guilt because they feel themselves to be unique—and inferior—in their sexual preferences and behavior.

Parents no longer live in a closed society. Victorian morals and habits might have insulated parents from the *overt* aspects of sexuality outside the permitted area of monogamous marriage, leavened for the male by dealings with prostitutes, but an open society like ours has no room for dirty secrets. On the contrary, where in Victorian society sexual repression fitted into the overall social scheme of accumulation, thrift, and postponed enjoyment, it does so no longer. Our society offers a material plenty—at least to some. And one consequence of that is the requirement that each of us accept the responsibility for making sexual and vocational choices, social and political commitments, a decision as to life-style, and, of course, independent thinking in all fields that concern the directing factors of life. Repression, which was perhaps useful in the nineteenth century, may become pathology in an open society, for it can place most severe and damaging pressures upon the individual.

Parents and children in a technological society can no longer afford to treat sexuality as their grandparents did. The doors must be open (indeed they already are). Old prejudices must be dealt with firmly so that they will cease to distort our lives.

The so-called sexual revolution is not a revolution, it is only a discovery of what sexuality really always has been. The more relaxed parents are in their own sexual life-style, the better will they be able to approach the sexual life-style of their children. Hiding and covering up are gone; the obscence giggle about sexuality should vanish, too. There is no need for hysteria about the ''sexually free'' or the dirty book on 42nd Street. Pornography is as much a part of sexuality as masturbation, and both have a useful place in the realm of sexuality. Parents as voters should once and for all put a halt to the efforts of what the late Fiorello La Guardia called the ''peanut politicians'' who try to regulate private sexuality and make loud noises about public morality while their own political morals make corruption commonplace and the neglect of real issues respectable. Cleaned-up newsstands only allow dealers to offer forbidden material at speculators' prices.

Above all, let parents and those who have something of a parental role in society remember that their tasks are to enlighten and to understand. It is not their job to restrict, to regulate, or to prescribe patterns of sexual behavior to children and teen-agers. Young people themselves, with the help and, hopefully, the insight of their elders, must explore and discover their own desires and their own ways of dealing with their sexuality so that, in the long run, it will be an enriching rather than a depleting element in their existence.

## II

The breakdown of the traditional sexual mores has profoundly affected the role of the father in contemporary society. Amazingly enough, too little attention has been given to this phenomenon. Too many psychoanalysts and sociologists are still concerned with (and writing about) the mother. The old clichés regarding the mother are still being repeated, and the role of the father in the sexual formation and education of children is virtually ignored. That the father's role has been affected by the changing sexual patterns is cause of concern. More and more children are detecting the defects in their fathers' role. They might even absorb many of the sexual difficulties that currently beset their once strong (and potent) fathers. The obvious increase in impotence among males has broader ramifications than the interaction between husband and wife and subsequently also affects the father's role and *image* of the first one in the family.

The old days have gone. The old ways are in flux. Nowhere is this more evident than in the dwindling position of the father. Once he was pictured as the authority in the home; now he is portrayed as its butt. This change is not entirely a contemporary phenomenon. Ever since the United States changed from an agricultural to an industrial economy—a change that began as early as the 1830s in the northeast—the father has been a joke: His economic mobility outstripped his social adaptability. While his wife and children attempted to adopt upper-middle-class manners and tastes, the father remained as he was born, stubbornly lower middle class. Seriously, in such novels as Howells's *Rise of Silas Lapham,* jeeringly, in a comic strip such as *Bringing Up Father,* the American nouveau riche father has been shown to be inept, clumsy, and ill at ease in the world. Smiles and sneers were also directed, however, toward his social climber of a wife and the pampered children who wanted to forget the world they had outgrown, momentarily at least. Father, for all his naïve informality or outright crudity stands firm; he is his old-fashioned self, retaining his established identity, as it were, rather than trying to develop a new identity better suited to life in the group into which his new wealth buys him entry.

In contrast to the attitudes that endured until the 1920s, today we hear little of the father's stubborn resistance to social grace and esthetic appreciation. Today we laugh at father's incapacity to govern his family. No longer does he command attention and deference by the mere sound of his voice. No longer does he exemplify success and achievement.[4] In fiction, particularly in the mass meda of comic strip and TV,

"Father Knows Best" only as sarcasm. He is the person who makes ludicrous blunders, especially in dealing with people, and who is rescued from the consequences of his ineptitude by his wife, or even by his adolescent son or daughter. Father has lost his traditional position in the family structure.

In compensation, perhaps, not he, but mother is held to blame if anything goes amiss in child rearing, especially if a child is emotionally disturbed. Patients in psychotherapy usually assume that their neuroses have grown out of their relationships with their mothers; any mention of father seems surprising to them. In many instances, only after the patient has spent some time in therapy does he begin to talk about his father, whether as a protective or antipathetic figure.[5] What could more vividly illustrate the erosion of the traditional father-son relationship?

Once father was, as a matter of course, a guide and model for his son; today, frequently, he neither has that function nor wishes to have it. When Kenneth Keniston looks at the family histories of his alienated young men, he tends to find that they have grown up in families where the father is seen as weak yet oppressive, responsible for confining a potentially talented mother to a dreary round of housewifery. That same "abused" mother manipulates father, nevertheless, so that alienated young men see their fathers to be foolish, false, and weak. Sometimes fathers seem absorbed in their families or at least in the houses and cars that they have bought to sustain a good life. As often, fathers who find their families disappointing as a source of emotional sustenance turn to their work. But that work, however compulsively it may be pursued, often yields only empty barrels for harvest.[6]

In contrast to the European middle-class father, the father in America often has become a stranger in his family. This, too, is no novel trend, but it may seem strange that the psychotherapist should see so much evidence of it at a time when leisure has supposedly increased, when middle-class parents are, by and large, so much younger than they used to be, and when one is deluged with talk about the revival of family living as a consequence of the postwar generation's exodus to the suburbs.

Perhaps contemporary leisure affects the middle class less than people at a lower income level. The blue-collar unionized workman and the white-collar office worker both have fixed and shrinking workweeks. People in typical middle-class occupations—business management and the professions—are not protected by union contract, by custom, or by employer willingness to make concessions in order to block unionization; here, long hours of work are expected (the three-hour lunch usually is at least nominally in pursuit of business not relaxation). Often business and social life are indistinguishable; "deals" are turned on the golf links or at the bridge table or in expense-account beds.

Fathers so occupied have little free time to give their children. The separation between father and son grows; spontaneity in the relationship is depleted by the emphasis on the external signs of masculinity. Fathers can no longer be physically close to their sons even if they do spend time in the boys' company. Again, this is not new: English and American manners have long held tenderness to be somewhat unmanly and have forbidden physical demonstrations of good feelings between men.* Even after long separation, Americans shake hands; the formal European kiss of greeting is suspect. Slaps on the back, digs in the ribs, punches are permissible, a quietly encircling arm elicits at least unspoken comment.

Longtime trends have become stronger in recent decades; an adolescent boy who walks arm-in-arm with his father may be regarded as odd, if not unmanly. On the other hand, fathers who refrain from an overt show of affection for their sons communicate the fear underlying that avoidance.

In this instance, the father does offer his son a model, but a model of neurotic fear and weakness rather than a model of manliness. The father has abdicated his authority; his wife now governs the home. A man

* I always have maintained that the physical ease with which French males encounter each other has contributed to the low rate of male homosexuality in that country.

may be willing to accept responsibility at work (although much is heard about the desire to avoid responsibility, even in business), but he prefers not to make decisions for the family. He may become friends with his sons; however, it is an undemanding surface friendship calling for little intimacy. The father is a pleasant companion, at times, but rarely is he willing to provide the image of stable maturity that his children need if they are to establish a secure, untroubled identity. Such reluctance to be fathers may be especially common today, when many middle-class men, married in their teens or early twenties, are as desperate as their wives in their efforts to conceal their age. Since paternity is too obvious to be denied, such fathers often try to mitigate it by playing peer to their adolescent children. Even at forty-plus, however, men may be reluctant to accept the father role. If children are unruly, unsuccessful at school, inept, or unpopular, father blames not them but their mother. Rarely does he assert his authority in order to change the situation, and when he does, it is often fruitless; he acts clumsily, self-consciously, because he is not behaving in the way he prefers. To be real head of the family, to act effectively as a father, the father must be an adult, but too many American fathers resist growing up.

Although some men cherish the external signs of masculinity to the verge of fetishism, although the red-blooded he-man is the ego ideal glorified by the mass media, although everything from automobiles to shaving lotion that a father may buy is marketed with the seal of approval of a broad-shouldered taper-waisted athlete whose muscles are evident under smoothly fitted evening clothes—in spite of all this, the contemporary American father is apt to be passive. And he does not want to be an adult upon whom his son can model himself; he is as much in need of mothering as his son.

The American father's refusal to accept his traditional place of primacy and authority in the family is closely related to his tendency to work himself into the kinds of stomach and heart disease that are very closely linked with the experience of stress. Why does the American middle-class father in this presumed age of leisure and affluence continue to center his existence around his job; why does he seem quite as submerged in his task as he was in the days of the seventy-two-hour work week?

Granted that the American middle-class family is costly, and that rising levels of expenditure require higher incomes to be won only by working or by speculation and financial manipulation, which are no less productive of worry and stress, there is, nevertheless, a devotion to work by many young executives that is not explained. At work they can apparently let themselves go, immersing themselves in their organizations or in their professions as they cannot do with their wives and children. Involvement with those a man is supposed to love and to be loved by poses far more of a threat to the young executive's psychological integrity and his identity than he feels in the grinding struggle of competition for advancement, success, and money. Indeed, it is sometimes quite clear in clinical experience that some men relate to their families only competitively: They become their children's rivals, particularly the rivals of their sons, for their wives' attention and affection.

The pseudo-peer that many a present-day father tries to be is no genuine substitute for the parent; rather the effort reflects a situation in which men are caught because they want a certain security of status that is to be had only by marrying and establishing families, without fully committing themselves to marriage and fatherhood. Such men do not want to be fathers, yet they are, in effect, forced to be; they dare not refuse to comply with the demands being made on them. They give token compliance, therefore; they marry, and sometimes divorce, and marry again. They beget children and maintain them. Sometimes, these rather unwilling fathers use their breadwinning role as a means of escaping real involvement in the family.

### III

One of the most remarkable books that appeared during the last decade was David Cooper's *The Death of the Family* [7] because for the first time, to my knowlege, a distinguished psychoanalyst questioned the total structure *and* philosophy of the contemporary family. The book in many ways is an example of the kind of questioning that is sorely needed in the discussion of where we are with family and childhood today.

Sociologists have been telling us for a long time that the nuclear family can no longer function *as if* it still was and is a traditional family, the kind of inner-directed family that David Riesman described for us in his study *The Lonely Crowd*. Many contemporary, and especially *urban*, families are now faced with a totally new set of mores, if there are any mores left at all.

Contemporary couples often exchange partners *; they are more open about their sexual affairs but also about their sexual difficulties. Trial marriage has become more of an accepted fact and often prevents the long and arduous ordeal of divorce. As Cooper has put it, ". . . the only evil of divorce is the prior evil of marriage," [8] which implies that the total structure of marriage *as* related to the nuclear family is now at stake and in question.

Many women and men are just becoming aware of their real sexual needs. How often in marriage and family situations are the partners *just* performing for performance sake. Couples who have been married for four or five years stop sleeping with each other or perfunctorily perform once a month—"What the hell!" The fact that most people, men and women alike, are attracted to more than one woman or man in their life is now being followed up in the practice of everyday life and perhaps for the better. But all of this has serious implications for the survival of the traditional family. Consequently, as Cooper believes, new forms of living together probably have to be instituted.

That Cooper has not yet written the sequel on the death of childhood is amazing, because it follows logically that the profound changes in the family already are affecting the child.

* One of my colleagues observed once to me that such an exchange was cheaper than the nineteenth-century mistress. And perhaps that is the solution for the middle class in America today.

Children, especially in this country, already are an example that they *too* have outgrown traditional concepts of childhood. I often wonder if there is such a thing as childhood left. Many children do resemble, at least in an outward performing sense, adults. Perhaps we are going back to the Middle Ages when all children were miniature adults and were treated as such!

Children no longer are sheltered from the emotional and sexual issues in the family. They instinctively know what is going on and can no longer fulfill the expectations of being the *innocent* child. That is gone forever and it is in that sense that childhood is dying. What is needed here is a reeducation of the parents and prospective parents. Are they willing and ready (and mature enough) to deal with this *kind* of child?

Interestingly enough few parents or married and unmarried couples have pondered these questions. The notion that perhaps they should not have children at all (because they really do not want to) is also a fact that should seriously be considered. Most married and unmarried couples still believe that they *should* have children. Why? I remember that years ago one of my male patients who happened to live with a lovely girl and functioned well in that kind of relationship was torn about the fact that he should have children. When in his analysis he discovered that he was just trying to fulfill a societal expectation, he was immensely relieved and decided that he really did not want children and so did his girl friend.

The implications of this discussion obviously are deeper than can be discussed here. But it is sufficient to say that our changing sexual mores will continue to affect not only the fate of the family but also the nature and performance of childhood.

The place sexuality holds in any world is certainly a matter of that world's awareness. How much awareness of sexuality was there, in America or anywhere else, when the mass media were practically nonexistent? In other words, in medieval times awareness of sexuality came verbally through talk of sin or of love, in sermons, in songs, in poetry, and the messengers of sexuality were the priests and the minstrel-poets who talked of carnal wickedness or worlds well lost for love. No books, newspapers, radio, or TV existed. Particularly, nothing existed that could profit by stimulating the sexual drive.

Yet, as Rattray Taylor has written, sexuality was quite free in early medieval times. It was the Church that put the brakes on, as it were, and Taylor argues that, although those brakes never operated well enough to keep the sexual vehicle on the straight and narrow paths of abstinence or monogamous marriage, it was able to exert an increasing control both by legal enactment and by implanting sufficient guilt to secure self-restraint by many thousands of people. This improved restriction on sex-expression exacted ". . . a mounting toll of perversion and neurosis. For whenever society attempts to restrict expression of the sexual drive more severely than the human constitution will stand, one or more of three things must occur. Either men will defy the taboos, or they will turn to perverted forms of sex, or they will develop psychoneurotic

THE MASS-MEDIA
ROLE IN THE
APPROACH TO
SEXUALITY

symptoms, such as psychologically caused illness, delusions, hallucinations, and hysterical manifestations of various kinds. The stronger personalities defy the taboos: the weaker ones turn to indirect forms of expression.'' [1]

Clerical commands and social taboos meant that there was *no real communication* about sexuality. Sin and love might be defined and discussed, as has been said, but today's clear definitions of sexuality were lacking. One might say that the lack of communication might perhaps have been better, since definitions and a greater awareness of sexuality have not always made it easier for men to cope with their sexuality.

A basic difficulty was created by the Judeo-Christian tradition, which operated to limit sexual expression for men and women alike but, in fact, perhaps most severely for women. The tradition allowed and then even honored marriage; it permitted prostitution to exist. But the very need for marriage meant that human beings were flawed and faulty, too weak and selfish to be celibate or ever faithful to their spouses. To James Thurber's satiric ''Is Sex Necessary?'' most of the medieval and early modern moralists might have replied, ''Necessary, yes; honorable, no.'' Romeo and Juliet were tragic, Chaucer's Wife of Bath was comic, but neither Shakespeare nor the earlier poet could take sexuality as a respected though ordinary part of life; sexuality had to be either funny or destructive when expressed.

Even in the nineteenth century discussion of sexuality was restricted to the realm of pathology and medicine. Whatever was written on sexuality in that time, and in the eighteenth century also, was either regressive or totally ignorant of the psychological facts. It was still colored if not riddled with guilt, with the belief that sex really was a dirty affair. Ignorance about sexuality brought on a wave of mental illness, as Taylor remarked. Neither information nor the means of spreading it were available to counter ignorance and backwardness. What better could one expect when even doctors could talk about masturbation as a cause of insanity?

Since physicians were the only people licensed to talk and write about sex (and then for audiences of their colleagues only), the mark of illness was set not only on the varieties of sexuality (perversions, if you will) but also on so-called normal sexuality. After all, what did people really know about sexuality? Even in the nineteenth century, what did they know about the techniques of sexual experience? Sexuality, in effect, was equated with heterosexual intercourse. Marriage was the only area in which sexuality could properly be expressed. All other aspects of sexuality were ignored or were unmentionable. Homosexuality was called "the sin man dared not name." In what terms did people talk of sex, then, for talk about it they must. Well, there was romantic love, the longing for the perfect, the ideal (and usually unsuitable) woman; the poets and composers of *Lieder* of the nineteenth century, such as Goethe and Schubert, were never tired of strumming strings of love unreturned, the lonely poet at the brook, the lover betrayed, the love triumphant. Women, incidentally, were not supposed to be sexual beings; they might be deceived or abandoned, they might even be withered, unpleasant old maids, but sexuality did not harry them—not even when they went on the streets.

Sexuality in the past was not only rather a male prerogative, it was *covert,* not to be mentioned except under the guise of romantic love. Today, after a half century struggle against censorship, sexuality has come out of the dark corners, no longer associated only with forbidden fruit, taboos, and a general climate of secrecy and suppression, of mental illness and psychopathology.

Release from censorship and a desire for profit have turned contemporary mass media—advertising, newspapers, plus radio and TV—to sexuality as a means of selling their product. And the media of the 1960s and the 1970s have reached, in terms of *open* and uninhibited sexuality, what is shown in Michael Feingold's review of some contemporary plays: "The actors clutch each other madly, adoring their colleagues' flesh. Athos' arm around D'Artagnan. The General's hand on Corralina's breast. Embracing, kissing, neck-biting, goosing. Tit-squeezing, groin-licking, buggery, 69. Man and woman, two men, threesies, group-gropes, daisy-chains, erotic friezes. Not only around and between scenes but during them. While two actors speak sticho-mythia, one sodomized the other; as a mother reminisces, her adult son suckles at her breast. . . . So it's all around; it's the now thing. But why is it? What's it for? Where is it going? And is it worth going there?'' [2]

But, one may ask, with Feingold, "Where is theater going?" Is this display of sexuality better than the nineteenth century when Krafft-Ebing and Lombroso explored sexual aberrations, while Freud, Jung, and Adler explored *psyche* and *soma;* when Victorian England found a scapegoat in Oscar Wilde, and the legislators of Kaiser Wilhelm's Germany lashed out against homosexuality in high places (see Chapter II, Part I), and the populace had its sexual morality reinforced by terroristic police enforcement of laws that even then were obsolete; when squeamish magazine and newspaper editors served prurience with horrified reports about the "white slave" traffic; and when self-appointed censors such as Boston's Watch and Ward Society punished publishers for printing novels whose language was too like that which men used in real life?

"Morality" was thus imposed with no genuine conviction, as the public scandals bear witness. We have ample evidence that the "social" context of life in the century of *transition* between the sordid utilization of the machine and the envisioned coming of automation was well suited to the most loathsome sexual hypocrisies. Society placed woman on a pedestal while it was exploiting maid servants and initiating entire generations of young men into sex by sending them to prostitutes.

A few works, such as Dumas's *Lady of the Camelias* or Ibsen's *Ghosts,* shed some artificial tears in a vain attempt to wash away the stains of a society that was as incapable of love as it was of eroticism. Equally in vain were its attempts to glamorize the world of prostitution by referring to the liberty of a vanished era in such works as Stendhal's *Henri Brulard,* Flaubert's *L'Education sentimentale,* and later, Celine's

*Death on the Installment Plan* or Henry Miller's *Tropic of Cancer*. Their vision of bawdy houses as the house of generosity is essentially subjective; their defiance of bourgeois morality is often an artist's safe moral coquettishness, such as we find in the admiration of Swinburne and Tennyson for Sade.

It was this nineteenth-century society, in which young men learned about sex from prostitutes, that would not tolerate Ingres's *"Turkish Bath,"* Courbet's *"Girl Friends,"* Carpeaux's *"Dance,"* or Manet's *"Lunch on the Grass."* Meanwhile, from 1850 on, photography had begun to cheapen "imitations of life" but was still held back from becoming an art in its own right by conventions as arbitrary as they were insufficient. With the advent of photography, however, examples of eroticism proliferated. In place of a drawing, miniature, painting, or a limited edition of an engraving, society is served by the techniques of photography, which make an unlimited number of pictures possible. Mass production and mass distribution provide their own antidote, since the plethora of images rapidly reaches the saturation point. Jayne Mansfield's bosom, captured on film while "accidentally" exposed in Rio, Las Vegas, Rome, or Hollywood, soon loses its shock value; even its potential to excite may diminish. Nevertheless, instead of facing the problem of graphic porno-eroticism, modern society approaches it with old habits of hypocrisy about sex; it even tries to conciliate commerce and morality, smoldering obsessions and politics, sexual *insatisfaction* and demagogy. The current apostles of decency organize great meetings of young people to counteract the public display of female affection and sexual service to rock and roll troupes and find that their good, proudly square specimens of adolescence are as ready for destructive boisterousness as their beaded and bearded contemporaries.

Long before this, however, the citadel of prudishness had gradually crumbled. World War I played its part. Since 1912 public display of the naked female (if not the male) has become acceptable under various pretexts, varying from the slow and stately movements imposed on nude Parisian showgirls to the "living-statute" immobility of London's revues and the obscene nipple-cups and G-strings of American burlesque. The brutal and banal exposure of flesh made eroticism democratic, offering its garish wares like a modern department store.

In 1913 Valentine de Saint Point published the *Futurist Manifesto of Lust,* which proclaimed "lust is the carnal searching for the Spiritual. . . . Art and War are the great manifestations of sexuality; lust is their flowering."

Put this manifesto beside the works of Havelock Ellis, which were its contemporary, and its literary facetiousness will be revealed. More recently, if we compare surrealist "contributions" to erotic theory, such as their 1929 "Inquest on Love" or Breton's "Mad Love," with the works undertaken by Maranon or the theses of René Guyon, we are forced to throw these poetical intuitions into limbo.

If the nineteenth-century censor prosecuted *Mme Bovary,* Charles Baudelaire, and Charles Leland (the author of *Hans Brinker or The Silver Skates,* a children's classic, who found his work halted by the law just as his polyglot five-language dictionary of slang approached the letter "F"), and if later publishers suppressed such mild expressions of sexuality as Dreiser's *Sister Carrie,* the mid-twentieth century was more realistic about sexuality. For all that puritanism had a brief revival in the Paris of Mme de Gaulle, such French novelists as George Bataille, Jean Genet, Pauline Reage, and Joyce Mansour contributed in large degree to that liberation.

Novelists no longer disguise sexuality but display it openly. Sexual conflicts, of whatever nature, are no longer avoided. Even in the United States movies show masturbation, homosexuality, and incest to say nothing of heterosexual intercourse discretely outside marriage. The theater, too, has gone a long way in displaying sexuality; lesbianism, sodomy, and other sexual diversions are all freely displayed on the stage. No variety of sexuality remains untouched, and why should it? If fetishism and sadism are a part of contemporary life, why not depict them in art—on the stage, in film, or in other mass media. Whether it be TV, radio, film, or newspapers, the mass media have rediscovered sexuality. Their use of sexuality—if only to sell soap and automobiles—has contributed to the slow erosion of sexual taboos. Now, if we have the will and the desire, we can face sexuality *as it is,* as part of the world in which we function.

Still, a considerable residue of sexual ignorance remains and continues to be exploited. The success of *Portnoy's Complaint,* which is no more than a boring recital of the masturbatory activities of a middle-class Jewish boy, strikes many people as revealing. To others, that belief is only a commentary on the slow pace of the general public's movement away from sexual ignorance.

Alan Friedman's *Willy-Nilly,* which describes a hermaphrodite who finally, through surgery, turns into a boy, is a much more genuine sign of progress. It shows how literature can comment on the place of sexuality in our lives. And this tale of transformation reveals more about our changing attitudes toward sexuality than a story about masturbation. [3]

No doubt the mass media will continue to exploit sexuality. No doubt books, too, will continue to help break open all the secret refuges of sexuality. Some of this may be more prurient display rather than honest exploration or equally forthright fun. But even exploitation must be tolerated, for only thus can society avoid the stultification of censorship and the resurgence of officially imposed restraint. In freedom alone can contemporary Americans come to terms with sexuality and find a path to a sexual morality appropriate to our time.

Adrian van Kaam remarked that many patients "experience a fundamental split between their sexuality and the other dimensions of their lives." [1] Although van Kaam speaks of sexuality in terms of patients in psychotherapy, the split between sex and the rest of existence is a phenomenon with which Western man has long been acquainted. Passion—and the word has usually meant sexual passion—has been distorting the schemes men laid out for their lives as early as the time described by Homer, when the Trojan Paris ran off with Helen, the King of Sparta's wife, and all Greece pursued, fighting a ten-year war and bringing a city to ruin. Sexuality has always pressed against the social rules, for those rules have usually been regulatory and restrictive and the sexual force they have tried to hold in check has found channels of sickness when the channels of health were blocked off. The integration of sexuality into one's life situation continues to be a central problem for twentieth-century man in his new mass society. The sense of sexuality as an alien aspect of the human self is a heritage of the Christian-Judaic tradition.

During recent decades not only psychoanalysts but even Christian philosophers, the French existentialist Maurice Merleau-Ponty, in particular, have emphasized sexuality as essentially an existential experience and *presence*. My body, as Merleau-Ponty says, is a subject. My body invests *my* world with meaning even before I think about this

PERSPECTIVE ON
SEXUALITY IN A
MASS SOCIETY

meaning. The body imposes a meaning on things that is not the imposition of meaning on the world by my consciousness.

The integration of sexuality into one's existence thus is fundamentally a unique, individual experience. Hence *all* notions—as laid down by external rules—about what human sexuality ought to be are irrelevant to the experience of a person's own unique sexuality. It is now clear that contemporary man's dealing with his sexuality is still plagued by biases inherited from the past that are distorting the present. For all that Freud and his followers did in at least showing that the sexual drive of men and women cannot safely be ignored, they too suffered from the same notions about sexuality as their less enlightened contemporaries. They too were caught in their own period; they accepted much of the restricted Victorian ideal of sexual morality. As persons, most of the early analysts regarded varieties of sexual behavior other than heterosexual genital intercourse as perversions of sexuality; they were culturally biased in their own attitudes toward sexuality.

Marie Bonaparte, following Freud, saw female sexuality ideally expressed in true women: normal, vaginal, maternal.[2] Both Freud and Marie Bonaparte obviously were the product of their nineteenth-century upbringing, where women were supposed to marry and become mothers. Were it not for Freud and Marie Bonaparte, some of these women might have failed to realize what vaginal satisfaction meant to them and how proper it was that they should have such satisfaction. Sexual development geared to a subordinated role in a husband-financed marriage was the status of the middle-class female in Freud and Marie Bonaparte's time.

Today, however, as middle-class women more and more must earn their own living in an organizational society that rests not on land but on commercial paper, many women no longer see their sexual norms in terms of maternity. In treating a substantial number of young women (age range 20–35) during the past decade, I have noticed a veering away from traditional concepts. More and more these women talk of their life situation in terms of accepting femininity and expressing their sexuality, but they do not necessarily wish to tie their lives for long periods to men they consider less than satisfactory. And although these young women are patients in therapy they are not basically different from many other young women of the same social level. And these women feel that their sexual expression should not necessarily be tied to the maternal instincts. They protest the dogma of a past that assigned women (and their sexuality) the prescribed social role of motherhood.

I never, incidentally, have fully understood why motherhood always has been stressed in urging marriage on women and fatherhood apparently never has been the overriding drive urging men to get married. Unless one accepts the notion that the maternal instincts are stronger in women than the fatherly instincts in men, traditional attitudes do not make much sense. Actually, there is little backing, other than philosophical and cultural speculations, which are merely products of the environment, for the idea that all women seek motherhood. Even the psychoanalyst Erik Erikson, who certainly cannot be accused of being backward in these matters, writes about "the central importance of woman's procreative task" and "her natural dispositions." [3] Here again normal female sexuality is, at least by implication, limited to what is considered the most important *creative* task of women.

Many women, however, refuse to accept such definitions; they want to experience their sexuality upon their own individual terms. David Riesman has written that postponement of full sexual experience was normal for the middle-class people of his mother's generation, but that the situation has changed.

> *The spread of affluence downward in the society and the greater confidence in one's long-run future that many college-educated people now possess, thanks to full employment for them, large organizations which seek them out, and a more meritocratic way of life, permits the middle class to depart from its earlier orientation toward saving, thrift, and* postponement *of grati-*

*fication. Installment buying is no longer confined to the impulsive lower class, and hedonism penetrates where pinched gentility once prevailed. Furthermore, affluence has meant not only the ability to enjoy now and yet get ahead, but a declining age of puberty as better nutrition has moved it steadily downward. And affluence also compels a far greater exposure to the lures of commercial vendors of sexuality, in which smoking a cigarette, putting on perfume, driving a car, and many other forms of consumer behavior have become sex-linked.* [4]

Contemporary mass society has no room for postponing gratification on any level. Neither males nor females are going to live by the sexual rules of the past. And so, in a sense, the situation all comes apart. Confrontation between male and female sexuality and between the demands of both is only beginning in this society. The person David Riesman calls the "affluent" housewife, who is shrewishly resentful of what she perceives as condescension from the woman of her own social and educational level who works outside her home, may well lead the way to sexual liberation.

Recognition of the diversionary role of sexuality has made many conventional married couples willing to "experiment," a willingness that can only increase in coming decades. I am not talking only about sophisticated "swinger clubs" and the poorly disguised orgies of the suburban middle class, but about the frustration of people faced with more permissive attitudes toward sexuality who simply do not know how to integrate that into their lives. Marriage in the traditional sense has already become an obstacle to the full exploration of sexuality. The pornography on 42nd Street is not being bought by swinging single men and women, but by young married folk living in a society where sexuality is constantly flaunted, where enjoyment is a social duty, where "sexual fulfillment" has become a commandment, and where, as a result, many people feel their matter-of-fact content in marriage has somehow given them less than they should be having. Thus, it is those who seem most embedded in "normality" who seek relief without wholly sacrificing their all-too-structured lives.*

To assume that only women have problems in terms of their sexuality is a major error; contemporary men have an even more difficult time coming to terms with their sexuality.[5] In a psychologically sophisticated society, men can no longer merely assert their masculinity. What a man thinks he is sexually and what comes through to the world may be very different; the loud-voiced sports fan may still seem an insecure and emasculated male. Men often see sexuality as something *outside* their own personality and they still may feel that they must respond to the obsolete traditional demands of a swiftly fading restrictive society. They still hide their sexual desires (except for such acceptable outlets as dirty jokes and double entendres) and their sexual problems. They fear impotence, aging, and often women themselves. Men express hostility toward homosexuality, which they cannot see as anything other than a threat *to them* rather than merely as another variety of sexual behavior. They put their sexuality into a separate compartment and seldom try to integrate sexuality into their whole life situation.

This brings us to the place of marriage in contemporary sexuality. Does the contemporary free recognition of sexuality threaten the institution of marriage? Although somewhat skeptical about traditional marriage, I agree with Edna Rostow: "'Romance is not dead, but there is an awareness that love as an impulsive feeling is not enough; that marriages may be made in heaven, but have to be lived on earth.'' [6] Yet society still has to realize more fully that marriage is only a part of the sexual lives of many men and women. Convention once might have restricted sexual expression to marriage (for women at least), but now

* A homosexual patient reported the reaction he received after placing an ad in *Pleasure* ( a New York underground newspaper) in which he asked males to contact him for possible homosexual experiences. He received 92 calls in the first two days. Of the 92 callers, 35 males identified themselves as married and wanting to experience something new.

sexuality has outgrown the confines of marriage. No longer is it possible or even desirable to institutionalize sexuality in the bounds of marriage. For many, marriage is a way in which to experience sexuality, but it also provides other important aspects of their lives: companionship, the joy of children, the anticipation and the realization of a shared lifetime. But all this has little or nothing to do with sexuality. People do experience affection and sex elsewhere than in marriage; they find lovers, friends, and companions outside the confines of marriage. For many marriage is merely a sexual convenience, a place where sex may be had safely and on demand. And it is at this point that many contemporary marriages are falling apart. No longer can sexuality be hidden to be experienced only in marriage. Husbands suddenly become aware that women other than their wives are attractive—why should he deny himself the pleasure of their company? Wives, and especially working wives perhaps, find other men attractive enough to make them resent the restrictions imposed by conventional morality. She might know, given the information and even the misinformation so abundantly available about sexuality, that the sex she may enjoy with her husband still may be a conventional experience, limited and lacking.

The more sexuality is written about, the more information seeps down to those who heretofore were ignorant about sexuality and sexual techniques, the more people come to feel that sexuality is both beautiful and their due, the more uneasy men and women become about their own sex lives, the more many couples realize what they may be missing. How many men are good lovers and know how to excite their wives? How many women are good lovers who know how to satisfy their husbands? How many men and women alike are still puritanical about what they do in bed with each other?

Continuous public discussion of sexuality has forced many men and women into confrontation with themselves and their values; they are compelled to reevaluate their sexual lives and situations.

Particularly, they are, or should be, forced to reevaluate some current ideas about their tasks as parents in relation to their children's sexual development. It continues to amaze me when I read that educators are talking about protecting children in terms of their growing sexuality. I, for one, believe that in the past—and a not-so-recent past at that—children simply grew up in ignorance of their sexuality; they *discovered* their sexuality on their own and through each other. There never was anything to protect on this level; there simply is nothing to protect. Victorian notions of the sexual ignorance of childhood were actually a sort of perversion, for they demanded that the child's "purity of mind" be protected by ignorance. Ignorance, however, protects nothing—except pathology, perhaps. Children, as well as adults, should be informed. The information should be full and straightforward, and it should *confront* children with their own sexuality.

Parents really do not talk with their children about sex, not even in contemporary society. In my clinical experience, I have not encountered one young patient, man or woman, who could truly say that he could communicate with his parents about sexuality. They had, of course, at a proper age, been told about "the facts of life," a phrase I consider rather foolish. To inform children about the biology of sex does not provide them with "the facts of life." Those facts embrace far more than sex, in the first place, and in the second, sexuality is an aspect of experience that is to be found only in the sexual *encounter* itself.

Sexuality is more than an instinct or drive. Sexuality involves *choice* —of partner, of behavior pattern, of attitude. Thus sexuality in *all* its aspects is part of our total life situation. We have graduated from pathology, from the reporting Hirschfeld and Krafft-Ebing. We have come through psychoanalysis and the statistics of sexual behavior. Men and women are entering a new epoch in the experience of sexuality in the world. Old conventions, old moralities will lose their hold, if they have not already done so; hence, we do well to be prepared to look at sexuality in a clear-eyed fashion and to deal with it frankly; it is no longer possible to repeat old puritanical catch phrases; those sound hollow, unrelated to the needs of our peculiarly dynamic society. Pornography, formal license for sexual behavior, moralizing about sexual habits—none of these need be dealt with as a "problem" since they all echo the past. Sexuality in the future will develop along other paths than those that have become traditional. The coming decades will be crucial for the development of a modern, healthy sexuality. The pill, abortion, and the sexual liberation of both men and women will not be considered a real problem. The true issue is how human beings are going to stand up in their ultimate confrontation with existence in a world where sexuality is taken for granted as part of life rather than as a dirty secret to be discussed in sniggering whispers or as a dangerous commodity to be dispensed only in the institution of marriage (or in prostitution, an institution developed at least partly to relieve the pressures of the first).

A liberated sexuality offers a field of action in which human potentiality for creative growth may be achieved. Can a mass society based on a marketing morality accommodate that potentiality? Or will sexuality, too, become a mere adjunct to selling soap? Glossy advertisements suggest a positive answer. But what alternative may be posed by the "saving remnant" of the deliberately unwashed?

INTRODUCTION

[1] To cite an example, Magnus Hirschfeld's monumental works *Sittenge-schichte des I. Welt Krieges* and *Sittengeschichte 1918–1933* have just recently been reissued by Verlag Karl Schustek, Hanau/Main, 1968.

[2] For an interesting work on some unconventional or "way-out" aspects of contemporary sexuality, see Gillian Freeman, *The Undergrowth of Literature* (London: Thomas Nelson, 1967).

[3] Even within Victorian society sexuality had its interesting aspects. Did not great scandals take place in that society? In reading Rupert Croft-Cooke's latest book *Feasting with Panthers* (London: W. H. Allen, 1967), which described some aspects of the lives of Swinburne, Symonds, and Wilde, I am not so sure that sexuality, although hidden, did not fundamentally affect their lives and those of their contemporaries.

[4] In reading Frank Feld's *The Last Days of Mankind: Karl Kraus and His Vienna* (New York: St. Martin's Press, 1967), I was struck by a statement of Kraus's: "A trial involving sexual morality is a deliberate step from individual to general immorality."

[5] Ghislain de Diesbach, *Secrets of the Gotha* (London: Chapman and Hall, 1967), p. 79.

[6] See J. J. Beljon, "Waar je Kijkt . . . Erotiek" (Amsterdam: Weten-schappelijke Uitgeverij, 1967).

[7] See Lars Ullerstam, *The Erotic Minorities* (New York: Grove Press, 1966).

[8] Especially in films we have seen sexual symbolism and overt sexuality in all its aspects. The films of Fellini and Warhol are a case in point. In our latest

**notes**

fashions feminine and masculine symbols have been stressed. Boots, leather, and flower-covered blouses for men are but a part of this process.

⁹ See my book *The Male Myth* (New York: Dell, 1967) and also the article "Masculinity in America" by Ralph A. Luce, Jr., in *The Psychoanalytic Review*, Vol. 54, No. 4, 1967.

¹⁰ Until a couple of decades ago there were still codes of sexual behavior prescribing the specific role of men and women. These codes certainly have not completely disappeared, but they are now much less taken for granted.

¹¹ I have noticed in contemporary patients who were perfectly secure in their heterosexual adjustment a distinct disappointment at not having experienced homosexual experiences.

¹² A notable exception is the Roman Catholic Church in Holland, which has been a pioneer during the last decades in the liberalization of sexuality. In particular, their sound approach toward homosexuality is remarkable.

¹³ For a recent study on desexualization in American life, see Charles E. Winick, *The New People* (New York: Pegasus, 1968).

CHAPTER 2

¹ Peter Gay, *Weimar Culture* (New York: Harper & Row, 1968), pp. 3–5. The Prince's outburst deserves to be recorded in German: "Heute abend in 'Hannele.' Ein grassliches Machwerk, sozialdemokratisch-realistisch, dabei von krankhafter, sentimentaler Mystik, nervenangreifend, uberhaupt scheusslich. Wir gingen nachher zu Borchard, um uns durch Champagner and Kaviar wieder in eine menschliche Stimmung zu versetzen."

² A question may be raised here: How much latent homosexuality was present in Wilhelm II? Certainly his almost pathological emphasis on masculinity indicates a deep insecurity about himself as a man. Surrounding himself with known homosexuals might have given him useful psychological reassurance, as well as a kind of vicarious participation in conduct that he thought he disapproved.

³ Maximilian Harden, "Fürst Eulenberg," in *Prozesse, Kopfe, Dritter Teil* (Berlin, 1913), pp. 182–183.

⁴ One is equally surprised that Eulenburg, a conspicuous homosexual, should enjoy the Emperor's intimacy or that Bismarck should reveal information that would discredit his ruler. Did the Chancellor actually know more about the Emperor's sexual tastes than anyone else or was he seeking revenge against a man who had usurped what he regarded as his own proper place in the Emperor's confidence?

⁵ Indeed there was, and curiously enough there still is, no vocabulary in

which one could talk about sex informally and without "obscenity." Between medical polysyllables and gutter simplicities, no words existed—a fact which of itself tells much about popular attitudes toward sex.

[6] See Magnus Hirschfeld, *et al., Sitten-Geschichte des Ersten Welt Krieges* (Hanau/Main, Verlag Karl Schustek, 1966; first edition, 1929); and *Zwischen Zwei Katastrophen-Sittengeschichte 1918–1933* (Hanau/Main, Verlag Karl Schustek, 1966; first edition, 1930); surprisingly, neither of these valuable books has been translated.

[7] Interestingly, Hirschfeld's homosexuality is mentioned in the unpublished *Rundbriefe* (the correspondence between Freud and his fellow psychoanalysts, members of the "Committee"). In a recent Dutch novel, Jaap Harten's *De Getatoeerde Lorelei* (Amsterdam, De Bezige Bij, 1968), Hirschfeld appears as an active, practicing homosexual. The novel, incidentally, gives an interesting insight into the sexual mores of Berlin in the 1920s. Another fictional treatment of the Berlin cultural and sexual scene in the '20s is Christopher Isherwood's *The Berlin Stories* (New York: New Directions, 1954).

[8] Berlin, 1914.

[9] Stuttgart, n.d.

[10] New York: Capricorn Books, 1965.

[11] Only two of Hirschfeld's books have been translated, *Sexual Anomalies and Perversions* (London and New York: Francis Aldor and Emerson Books, 1944); *Sexual Pathology* (New York: Emerson Books, 1940).

[12] His admission to the Society is discussed in the *Rundbriefe* (the unpublished correspondence between Freud and the members of the Committee). For the organization of the Committee, see Ernest Jones, *The Life and Work of Sigmund Freud,* Vol. II; and also my forthcoming book *The Seven Rings* .

[13] A recent edition of *Psychopathia Sexualis* has an excellent introduction by Ernest van den Haag (New York: Putnam, 1965).

[14] See his well-known *Sexual Life in England: Past and Present* (London: Arxo, 1958).

[15] See his learned study on sexual odor, *Odoratus Sexualis,* recently issued in this country (Brandon House, 1967).

[16] For an interesting discussion on the work of Moll, see *The Minutes of the Vienna Psychoanalytic Society,* Vol. II (New York: International Universities Press, 1967), p. 43. This volume also contains interesting references to the work of Sadger, who was an active member of the Vienna Psychoanalytic Society.

[17] Freud and Stekel are discussed in Chapter IV: Freud and Sexuality. For some of Stekel's excellent pathographies, see *The Minutes of the Vienna Psy-*

*choanalytic Society,* Vols. I and II (New York: International Universities Press, 1962, 1967). Incidentally, these volumes contain interesting sexual pathographies by Isidor Sadger. Sadger took quite an active part in the Wednesday evening meetings of the Vienna Psychoanalytic Society. Nunberg and Federn comment on Sadger in *The Minutes,* Vol. I, "Isidor Sadger belongs to the first and most gifted pioneers of psychoanalysis. Little is known about his personal life. Because of personality difficulties he became more and more isolated in the course of the years and finally disappeared during World War II. His contributions to the understanding of the perversions, particularly of homosexuality, are outstanding" (p. xxxvi).

[18] Readers interested in the cultural climate of nineteenth-century Vienna should read Ilsa Barea, *Vienna* (New York: Knopf, 1966). Also Alfred Schick "The Vienna of Sigmund Freud," *The Psychoanalytic Review,* Vol. 55, No. 4, 1968–69, pp. 529–551 and also Frank Field, *The Last Days of Mankind: Karl Kraus and His Vienna* (New York: St. Martin's Press, 1967).

CHAPTER 3

[1] An example is John Addington Symonds, who published his *A Study in Greek Ethics and A Study in Modern Ethics,* anonymously. One might also cite *My Secret Life,* which describes aspects of nineteenth-century sexual life in England. The man responsible for drawing attention to *My Secret Life* is Stevan Marcus, whose *The Other Victorians* is an outstanding study of the social implications of nineteenth-century English pornography.

[2] A good description of the group around Oscar Wilde is given in *Reggie, A Portrait of Reginald Turner* by Stanley Weintraub (New York: George Braziller, 1965) and in *Bosie* by Rupert Croft-Cooke (New York: Bobbs-Merrill, 1963). For a description of the Bloomsbury group, its goddesses, Vanessa Bell and Virginia Woolf, and its half gods, Maynard Keynes, Roger Fry, Clive Bell, and Lytton Strachey, see Michael Holroyd, *Lytton Strachey* (New York: Holt, Rinehart, and Winston, 1968).

An interesting account of some classic works of pornography is found in *Secrets of the British Museum* by Peter Fryer (New York: Citadel, 1968).

[3] Elisabeth Longford, *Victoria R.I.* (London: Weindenfeld and Nicolson, 1964), p. 394. The letter is also quoted in David Duff, *Hessian Tapestry* (London: Frederick Muller, 1967), p. 169.

[4] For an interesting account of Victoria's affair with John Brown, see *The Empress Brown* by Tom Cullen (Boston: Houghton Mifflin, 1969).

[5] Stella Margetson, *Leisure and Pleasure in the Nineteenth Century* (London: Cassell, 1969), pp. 68–69.

[6] I am indebted to Peter Fryer, who developed this notion in *The Man of Pleasure's Companion* (London: Arthur Barker, 1968).

[7] *British Medical Journal,* 1866, Vol. I, p. 186.

[8] *Dictionary of National Biography,* Vol. 12, p. 163.

[9] Fryer, *op. cit.,* p. 11.

[10] Havelock Ellis, *My Life* (London, 1940; Neville Spearman Ltd., 1967), pp. 362–363.

[11] *Ibid.,* p. xxx.

[12] Vincent Brome, "Sigmund Freud and Havelock Ellis," *Encounter* (March, 1959), pp. 46–53.

[13] This letter appears in *Letters of Sigmund Freud,* selected and edited by Ernst Freud (New York: Basic Books, 1960), pp. 380–381.

[14] Joseph Wortis, *Fragments of an Analysis with Freud* (New York: Bobbs-Merrill, 1963), p. 30.

[15] Ellis, *op. cit.*

[16] I am indebted to Samuel Hynes's study *The Edwardian Turn of the Mind* (Princeton: Princeton University Press, 1968) for some of the information contained in this chapter.

[17] Richard von Krafft-Ebing, *Psychopathia Sexualis* (Philadelphia and London, F. A. Davis Co. and F. J. Rebman, 1893), p. v.

[18] Ellis, *op. cit.,* p. 363.

[19] "The Question of Indecent Literature," *Lancet* (November 19, 1898), p. 1344.

[20] London *Times,* November 22, 1913, p. 11.

[21] Agnes Baden-Powell, in collaboration with Lt. Gen. Sir Robert Powell, *The Handbook for Girl Guides* (London: Thomas Nelson, 1912), p. 340.

CHAPTER 4

[1] James Strachey, ed., *The Standard Edition of the Complete Psychological Works of Sigmund Freud,* Vol. VII, (London: Hogarth Press and the Institute of Psychoanalysis, 1953), p. 12.6.

[2] Ernest Jones, *The Life and Work of Sigmund Freud,* Vol. II (New York: Basic Books, 1955), p. 286.

[3] Stendhal, *The Life of Henri Brulard* (New York: Vintage Books, 1955), pp. 29–30.

[4] See *Childhood and Society* (New York: W. W. Norton, 1955) and *Young Men Luther* (New York: W. W. Norton, 1958), and my own study on identity, *The Individual and the Crowd: A Study of Identity in America* (New York: Mentor Books, 1965).

[5] Bruno Bettelheim, "The Problem of Generations," *Daedalus* (Winter, 1962).

[6] Jean-Paul Sartre, *Critique de la raison dialectique,* I (Paris: Gallimard, 1960), p. 46.

[7] *Ibid.,* p. 49 (Sartre's italics).

[8] See my study *Freud and America* (New York: Macmillan, 1966).

[9] We are pleased that the Institute for Sex Research at Indiana University is conducting the first scientific study on homosexuality. See also my recent book *Homosexuality: A Changing Picture* (New York: Humanities Press, 1974).

[10] Sigmund Freud, *Three Contributions to the Theory of Sex* (New York: E. P. Dutton, 1962), p. 34.

[11] Irving Bieber, *et al., Homosexuality: A Psychoanalytic Study* (New York: Basic Books, 1962).

See also *The Gay World* by Martin Hoffman (New York: Basic Books, 1968), which is a far more responsible study of homosexuality than Bieber's.

[12] We are fortunate to have the minutes of these meetings for 1906–1910 available in an edition by Herman Nunberg and Ernst Federn (2 vols.; New York: International Universities Press, 1962, 1967).

[13] Alfred Schick, "The Vienna of Sigmund Freud," *The Psychoanalytic Review,* Vol. 55, No. 4 (1968–69), p. 533.

[14] *Minutes of the Vienna Psychoanalytic Society,* Vol. II (New York: International Universities Press, 1967), pp. 43–52.

[15] *Ibid.,* p. 45.

[16] Wittels's book was published in 1909 and has not been translated into English. Its theme is "Man must give free rein to his sexuality, or else he becomes crippled." Professor Ehrenfeld was an Austrian philosopher. His *Sexual Ethik* was published in 1907.

[17] *Minutes, op. cit.,* p. 86.

[18] *Ibid.,* pp. 89–90.

[19] *Ibid.,* p. 82.


CHAPTER 5

[1] Frederick Lewis Allen, *Only Yesterday: An Informal History of the Nineteen-Twenties* (New York: Blue Ribbon Books, 1932), p. 98.

[2] See H. M. Ruitenbeek, *Freud and America* (New York: Macmillan, 1966).

[3] Alfred C. Kinsey, Wardell B. Pomeroy, Clyde E. Martin, and Paul H. Gebhard, "Concepts of Normality and Abnormality in Sexual Behavior" in

*Psychosexual Development in Health and Disease,* Paul Hoch and Joseph Zubin, eds. (New York: Grune and Stratton, 1949).

[4] *Ibid.,* p. 32.

[5] See his study on homosexuality, Hans Giese, *Der homosexuelle Mann in der Welt* (Stuttgart: Ferdinand Enke Verlag, 1958). See also his *Psychopathologie der Sexualität,* 3 vols. (Stuttgart: Ferdinand Enke Verlag, 1959, 1960, 1962).

[6] See V. E. von Gebsattel, *Prolegomena einer medizinischen Anthropologie* (Berlin: Springer Verlag, 1954).

[7] Helmut Schelsky, *Soziologie der Sexualität* (Hamburg: Rowohlt, 1955).

[8] Max Scheler, *Wesen und Form der Sympathie* (Bonn: 1923), p. 233.

[9] *Von der "Psychopathia Sexualis" zur Sexualwissenschaft,* (Stuttgart: Ferdinand Enke Verlag, 1959).

[10] See Medard Boss, *Meaning and Content of Sexual Perversions* (New York: Grune and Stratton, 1949).

[11] Quoted in *Newsweek,* November 13, 1967, p. 75.

[12] Alfred Kinsey, *et al., Sexual Behavior in the Human Male* (London and Philadelphia: Saunders, 1948) and *Sexual Behavior in the Human Female* (London and Philadelphia: Saunders, 1953).

[13] Paul Ricoeur, ''Wonder, Eroticism and Enigma,'' *Cross Currents* (Spring, 1964).

CHAPTER 6

[1] Sigmund Freud, *Three Contributions to the Theory of Sex* (New York: Dutton, 1962; paperback).

[2] See Jacob A. Arlow, ''Perversion: Theoretical and Therapeutic Aspects'' in *Psychotherapy of Perversions,* Hendrik M. Ruitenbeek, ed. (New York: Citadel Press, 1967), p. 56.

[3] See W. H. Gillespie, ''Notes on the Analysis of Sexual Perversion'' in *ibid.,* p. 26.

[4] *Ibid.,* pp. 39–40.

[5] For an account of sadistic and homosexual involvement, see Warner Muensterberger, ''Perversion, Cultural Norm and Normality'' in *ibid.,* p. 99.

[6] *The Justice Weekly,* published in Canada, prints numerous advertisements geared to the needs of the sexually perverse; the Chicago *National Informer* directs ads to a similar audience. But material calculated to draw the attention of the knowledgeable to their opportunities also appears in newspapers and magazines that appeal to the general public.

[7] *Le vice Anglais* stands for the involvement with sadomasochistic activities,

especially flagellation. The term, incidentally, is not a synonym for homosexuality as some writers have assumed.

[8] Ivan Bloch, *The Sexual Life of Our Time* (London: Rebman, 1908), gives a scholarly account of the varieties of perverse sexual behavior of nineteenth-century England. More recent books on the subject are available but, too often, they are less informative than appealing to the appetite for sensation; R. C. van Yelyr, *The Whip and the Rod* (London: Gerald G. Swan, 1941) is a case in point.

[9] Neither they nor his unfinished novel *Lesbia Brandon* is included in his collected works, of course. This aspect of Swinburne is discussed in his latest biography, *Swinburne's Literary Career and Fame,* by C. K. Hyder (New York: Russell and Russell, 1963).

[10] There does, however, seem to be a good deal of clinical evidence for fetishism and exhibitionism as characteristic of male behavior. Heterosexual as well as homosexual males are given to fetishism. Currently, some homosexuals seem to show a great desire to display their fetishistic tendencies by wearing high boots and leather clothing, for example.

[11] Unconscious homosexuality in organizations like the Boy Scouts is described, in a fictionalized way, in *Eros: An Anthology of Male Friendship* (New York: Citadel Press, 1963), pp. 370–371.

[12] See Part I, Chapter II of this book.

[13] Elie A. Cohen, *Human Behavior in the Concentration Camp* (New York: Universal Library, 1961), p. 233.

[14] Roehm had been one of Hitler's earliest followers and was head of the SA when he was killed. His execution was political rather than moral in inspiration, however; Hitler wanted to be rid of a potential rival.

[15] See Ernest van den Haag, "Notes on Homosexuality and Its Cultural Setting" in Hendrik M. Ruitenbeek, *The Problem of Homosexuality in Contemporary Society* (New York: E. P. Dutton, 1963).

[16] Colin Wilson's *The Origins of the Sexual Impulse* (New York: G. P. Putnam's Sons, 1963) may be cited as an instance, although it is useful in some respects.

CHAPTER 7

[1] E. Gley, "Les aberrations de l'instinct sexuel," *Revue philosophique,* pp. 17, 66 (1884).

[2] Marie Bonaparte, Anna Freud, and Ernst Kris, eds., *The Origins of Psychoanalysis by Sigmund Freud* (New York: Doubleday Anchor), pp. 37–38.

³ G. Herman, "Genesis, das Gesetz der Zeugung," in *Libido und Mania* (Leipzig, 1903).

⁴ R. von Krafft-Ebing, "Zur Erklärung der contraren Sexualempfindung," *Jahrbuch Psychiat, Neurol.*, 13, 1 (1895).

⁵ *The Standard Edition* of the *Complete Psychoanalytical Works of Sigmund Freud* (London: Hogarth Press), Vol. VII, p. 141.

⁶ Sandor Rado, *Psychoanalysis of Behavior* (New York: Grune and Stratton, 1956), p. 139.

⁷ *Ibid.*, p. 140.

⁸ *Ibid.*, pp. 140–141.

⁹ *Ibid.*, p. 141.

¹⁰ *The Standard Edition*, Vol. XXII, *op. cit.*, p. 115.

¹¹ F. R. Lillie, "General Biological Introduction" in E. Allen, ed., *Sex and Internal Secretions* (2nd ed.) (Baltimore, Md.: Williams and Wilkins, 1939).

¹² Rado, *op. cit.*, p. 145.

¹³ *Collected Papers*, Vol. V (New York: Basic Books, 1959), p. 347.

¹⁴ See Medard Boss, *Meaning and Content of Sexual Perversions* (New York: Grune and Stratton, 1949).

¹⁵ Judd Marmor, ed., *Sexual Inversion* (New York: Basic Books, 1965), p. 242.

¹⁶ See André Gide, *Corydon* (New York: Farrar, Straus, 1950).

¹⁷ Hendrik M. Ruitenbeek, ed., *Homosexuality and Creative Genius* (New York: Astor-Honor Books, 1967), p. 265.


CHAPTER 8

¹ Irving Bieber, *et al.*, *Homosexuality, A Psychoanalytic Study* (New York, Basic Books, 1962).


CHAPTER 9

¹ Wilhelm Stekel, *Sexual Aberrations*, Vol. II (New York: Grove Press, 1964), pp. 3, 319.

² Sigmund Freud, *The Standard Edition*, Vol. XXI, p. 152.

³ Karl Abraham, "Remarks on the Psychoanalysis of a Case of Foot and Corset Fetishism" in *Selected Papers* (New York, Basic Books, 1953).

⁴ Sandor Lorand, "Fetishism in Statu Nascendi," *International Journal of Psychoanalysis*, Vol. XI, 1930.

⁵ Ernest Becker, *Angel in Armor* (New York: George Braziller), pp. 14, 16–17.

[6] Sigmund Freud, "Three Contributions to the Theory of Sexuality," *Standard Edition*, Vol. VII.

[7] Compare J. Layard, "The Incest Taboo and the Virgin Archtype," *Eranos Jahrbuch*, 12 (1945), 753. We look upon our work as being the foundation to these "central complexes" of the psychoanalytic theory; however we must not mistake it as a substitute for the therapeutic necessity to work out and make conscious to the individual these complexes through the process of psychoanalytic treatment. For general existential constituents become personal experience only in their concrete individual form. And only what we live through ourselves is therapeutically effective.

[8] Only if we understand that the ontologic basis of the arch-anxiety is related to our being-in-the-world and that this anxiety carries identity in its two forms (anxiety of having to-be-in-the-world and about being-in-the-world) can we conceive of the seemingly paradoxic phenomenon that people who are afraid of living are also especially frightened of death.

[9] Compare P. Schilder, *Das Zerstueckelungsmotiv*, Allg. aerztl. Zeitschr, f. Psychotherapie, I:23. Concerning the phenomenon of the so-called loss of soul, see D. P. Schreger; *Denkwuerdigkeiten eines Nervenkranken*, 1903, and G. J. Frazer, *The Golden Bough*, II (The Perils of the Soul) (London, 1911), p. 26.

[10] Compare the analogous situation of a female fetishistic pervert in H. von Hug-Hullmuth, *Ein Fall von weiblichem Fuss, richtiger Stiefelfetischismus*. Int. Zeitschr, f. Psychoanalysis, Vol. 3, 1915.

[11] Binet, "Du Fetichisme Dans L'Amour," *Revue Philosophique*, 1887; also Freud, *Drei Abhandl. zur Sexualtheorie*. Ges. Schr., V:27, and Vorlesungen z. Einfuehrung in die Psychoanalyse. Ges. Schr., VII:361.

[12] Sigmund Freud, *Drei Abhandl. zur Sexualtheorie*, Ges. Schr. V:28, footnote 1; also "Fetischismus," Ges. Schr. XI:396.

[13] Compare Schulz-Henke, *Der gehemmte Mensch* (Leipzig, 1940), p. 211, and M. Boss, *Die Gestalt der Ehe* (Bern, 1945), p. 34.

[14] I have not encountered actual cases of homosexual leather fetishists, but *Justice Weekly* (published in Canada) prints many ads for the homosexual fetishist. It is also well known that such homosexuals have their own "leather bars," where they meet.

CHAPTER 10

[1] One of the best essays on Sacher-Masoch appeared in Dutch by the Dutch author Alfred Kossman, *Martelaar voor een Dagdroom* (Amsterdam: Donker, 1962). Also James Cleugh's study *The Marquis and the Chevalier* (1951), which deals both with de Sade and Sacher-Masoch, is outstanding.

² In various cheap paperback publications such as *The Spankers, The Erotic Compulsive,* and *The Sexual Rebellion of the Sixties,* there is evidence that many passive men seek out sadistic, dominant women.

³ See *Chastisement* by John Barby (Brandon House, 1966).

⁴ Leslie Schaffer, ''Violence and the Failure of Invention,'' *Review of Existential Psychology and Psychiatry,* Vol. VIII, No. 3 (Fall, 1968), pp. 191–192.

CHAPTER 11

¹ James Cleugh, *Love Locked Out* (London: Anthony Blond, 1963).

² *Dialoog,* a Dutch homosexual publication, a couple of years ago organized with great success some weekends for parents of homosexuals.

³ Paul Ricoeur, ''Wonder, Eroticism and Enigma,'' *Cross Currents,* Spring, 1964.

⁴ In his *Brief an den Vater* Kafka describes the old-fashioned and self-righteous father in the following words: ''Deine Meinung war richtig, jede andere war verrückt, überspannt, meschugge, nicht normal. Dabei war Dein Selbstvertrauen so grosz, dasz Du nicht konsequent sein musztest und doch nicht aufhörtest recht zu haben.''

⁵ See Norman Kelman, ''Social and Psychoanalytic Reflections on the Father,'' in Hendrik M. Ruitenbeek, ed., *Psychoanalysis and Social Science* (New York: E. P. Dutton, 1962), p. 128.

⁶ Kenneth Keniston, *The Uncommitted: Alienated Youth in American Society* (New York: Harcourt, Brace & World, 1965).

⁷ David Cooper, *The Death of the Family* (New York: Pantheon, 1970).

⁸ *Ibid.,* p. 49.

CHAPTER 12

¹ G. Rattray Taylor, *Sex in History* (New York: Ballantine Books, 1954), pp. 22–23.

² Michael Feingold, ''Commedia, Clutching, FUTZ! and Fun,'' in *Yale Theatre:* ''Sex and the Single Theatre'' (Winter, 1968), p. 21.

³ Alan Friedman, ''Willy-Nilly'' in *New American Review,* II, p. 15.

CHAPTER 13

¹ Adrian van Kaam, ''Sex and Existence,'' in Hendrik M. Ruitenbeek, ed., *Sexuality and Identity* (New York: Delta Books, 1970).

² See Sigmund Freud, *Female Sexuality,* Standard Edition, Vol. XXI,

p. 225, and also Marie Bonaparte, *Female Sexuality* (New York: Grove Press, 1962), p. 1.

[3] Erik H. Erikson, "Reflections on Womanhood" in *Daedalus* (Spring, 1964), p. 605.

[4] David Riesman, "Two Generations," in *Daedalus* (Spring, 1964), p. 723 [italics mine (hmr)].

[5] I have touched upon this problem in more detail in my book *The Male Myth* (New York: Dell, 1967).

[6] Edna G. Rostow, "Conflict and Accommodation," *Daedalus* (Spring, 1964), p. 737.

Abnormalities, sexual. *See* Normalities vs. abnormalities; Perversion, sexual
Abortion, 120-121, 146
Abraham, Karl, 101
Academy of Medicine, New York, 26
Acton, William, 31
Adler, Alfred, 42, 135
Adolescence, 45-46, 63
    Bettelheim quoted on pressures, 46
    problems of, arising from modern family situation, 87-90, 124-129
    routes to homosexuality, 87, 90
    sexual identity crisis, 45-46, 90-91
Advertising, use of sex in, 44, 62, 63, 134, 138, 146
*Affirmations* (Ellis), 34
Aggression, in sex, 112-113
"Agony columns," 71-72
Albert, Prince Consort, 31
Alexander II, Tsar, 30
Alfred, Prince of England, 30

Algolagnia, 112
Alice, Princess of Hesse, 30
Alienists, 24
"Analysis Terminable and Interminable" (Freud), 78-79
Andreas-Salomé, Lou, 14
Anthropologic theory of perversion, 109-110
Anxiety, primal, 105, 106-107
Army life, 73
"Art" photography, 12
Arts:
    display of sexuality in, 136-137
    19th century prudery toward, 136
    sexual symbolism in, 3
Ashbee, Henry Spencer, 31
Association theory of perversions (Binet), 107-108
*Auf Bienchens Flügeln* (Ulrichs), 18n.
Austria, pioneers in sexology, 23, 25, 28, 51-54
Autoeroticism, 36
Axelrad, Sidney, 69

# index

Baden-Powell, Lady Agnes, 39, 40
Baden-Powell, Sir Robert, 39, 40
Bak, Robert, 68
Bataille, George, 137
Baudelaire, Charles, 137
Beauvoir, Simone de, 114, 115, 116
Becker, Ernest, 101-102, 110
Beljon, J. J., quoted, 2-3
*Berdache,* 71
"Berkeley Horse" flagellating machine, 72
Berlin:
> Institute of Sexual Science, 25-26
> of 1920's, fetishism and flagellation, 73
> Psychoanalytic Society, 26
Bettelheim, Bruno, 46
Bible, 9
Bieber, Irving, 50, 96
Big Nambas, 69
Binet, Alfred, 107-108
Birth-control pill, 63, 120-121, 146
Bisexuality, 75-81
> biological basis discounted, 78, 81
> as biological phenomenon, 75-76
> danger of concept, 79-81
> Freud and, 75-76, 77-79, 80
> Krafft-Ebing's hypothesis of neuro-psychological aspects of, 76, 77
> in literature, 80
> mask of, famous case examples, 79-80
> and neuroses, 76, 80
> and physical hermaphroditism, 76-77

rejection of theory, 78-79, 80-81
Bismarck, Prince Otto von, 16, 20-21
Bloch, Ivan, 12, 13, 23, 25, 26-27, 37
Bloomsbury, 30
Böhme, Jacob, 28
Bonaparte, Marie, 140
Books. *See* Literature
Boss, Medard, 102, 103
Boston, Watch and Ward Society of, 135
Boy Scouts, 40
Breton, André, 137
Breuer, Josef, 55
Brill, A. A., 26
*Bringing Up Father* (comic strip), 125
Britain:
> early sexologists, 33-41, 61
> Edwardian era, 35, 36, 39
> Labour Party, 41
> sadomasochism as "le vice Anglais," 17, 72
> sexual deviations, 17-18, 72
> Victorian society, 11-12, 30-33, 36, 39, 135. (*See also* Victorian era)
British Medical Association, 38
Brophy, Brigid, 116
Brothels, 10
Brown, John, 31
Burlesque, 137
Burroughs, William S., 3
Butler, Samuel, 11
Byron, George Gordon, Lord, 28

Camus, Albert, 115
Carpeaux, Jean Baptiste, 136
Carpenter, Edward, 33, 38-39, 40
> writings of, 38-39

*Castle, The* (Kafka), 115
Castration complex, 68, 90, 105-106,
  108
Catamites, 19
*Causes and Prevention of Immorality
  in Schools, The* (Lyttelton), 39-40
Céline, Louis Ferdinand, 135-136
Censorship, 133-134, 135, 137, 138
  of Bloch's books, 37
  of Ellis's books, 37
  of Freud's books, 38
  of pornography, effects of, 33,
    124
Chaucer, Geoffrey, 133
"A Child is Being Beaten" (Freud),
  50, 113
Childhood, 120 and n., 130-131
  ego splitting, 68
  and "facts of life," 52, 145
  Freudian libido, 43, 47
  Freudian theory of psychosex-
    ual development in, 43, 57
  "innocence," 43, 120, 131,
    145
  Kinsey on sexual development
    in, 57-58
  roots of fetishism, 107-108
  Sartre quoted, on sex role
    fixation in, 47-48
  sex education in, 119-124,
    144-145
  Stendhal quoted, on love for his
    mother, 43-44
  *See also* Adolescence; Family;
    Father-son relationship; In-
    fantile sexuality; Mother-
    child relationship; Mother-
    son relationship
Christian morality, 69-71, 133, 139

decline of, 2-3, 9
Churches, attitudes toward sex, 5,
  120, 132-133
*City and the Pillar, The* (Vidal), 85
Clothing, sexual symbolism in, 3, 110
Code Napoleon, 10, 59
Cohen, Elie A., 73
College fraternity initiation rites, 71
Commercialism, use of sex in, 44, 62.
  *See also* Advertising
*Contemporary Sexual Life* (Bloch), 12
"A Contribution to the Study of the
  Origin of Sexual Perversions"
  (Freud), 50
Cooper, David, 129, 130
Coote, Holmes, 32
Corporeal punishment, 70
Corpun Society, 70
Courbet, Gustave, 136
Courtesans, 10
"Cover memory," 108
*Crime and Punishment* (Dostoevsky),
  13
"A Critical Examination of the Con-
  cept of Bisexuality" (Rado), 76
Culkin, Father John M., 61
Culturalist school of psychoanalysis,
  49, 50, 51
*Curious Sex Customs in the Far East*
  (Hirschfeld), 26


"Dance" (Carpeaux), 136
Darwinism, 11
Daseinanalysis, 103, 105. *See also*
  Existential school of psycho-
  analysis
*Death of the Family, The* (Cooper),
  129

*Death on the Installment Plan*
(Céline), 136
Desexualization, 6
Development of sexuality:
    Freudian theory, 43, 46-47, 50,
        55, 57
    Kinsey's view, 57-58
    oral-phallic ego splitting in, and
        perversion, 68
    role of stimuli in, 57-58
Devereux, George, 69
Dilke, Sir Charles, 10
Divorce, 87, 130
    Carpenter's defense of, 39
    increase in, around 1900, 13
    19th century, 10
*Donovan's Brain* (film), 70
Dostoevsky, Fedor, 13
Dreiser, Theodore, 137
Dumas, Alexandre, 135
Duncan, Isadora, 12
Dutch suffragettes, 12


"The Economic Problem of Maso-
    chism" (Freud), 50
Eder, David, 38
*L'Education sentimentale* (Flaubert),
    135
Edward VII, King of England, 23
Edwardian era, 35, 36, 39
Ego splitting, 68
Egopsychology, 49
Ehrenfeld, Christian Freiherr von,
    52-53
*Elective Affinities* (Goethe), 13
Ellis, Havelock, 12, 33-38, 39, 40-41,
    55, 59, 61, 137
    and bisexuality, 77

marriage of, 34
*Sexual Inversion,* 37
studies of homosexuality, 36,
    37, 74
*Studies of the Psychology of
    Sex,* 34-35, 36-37, 50, 61
various writings of, 33, 34
England. *See* Britain
Erikson, Erik H., 45, 141
*Erotic Minorities, The* (Ullerstam), 3
Erotica, 33. *See also* Pornography
Eroticism, mass production and dis-
    tribution of, 136-138
*Erotische Weltbild, Das* (Hirschfeld),
    26
Ethics, sexual, 26, 27
Ethnology, sexual aspects of, 26
Eulenburg, Albert, 23, 27
Eulenburg und Hertefeld, Prince
    Philip zu, 20-22, 73
Europe:
    contemporary sexology, con-
        tinued notion of sexual per-
        version in, 59, 60, 62
    early sexology, *see* Austria; Bri-
        tain; Germany
    father role, compared to U.S.,
        126-127
    U.S. women compared to, 89
Existentialism, 98
Existentialist school of psycho-
    analysis, 47, 49, 60, 79, 92
    and fetishism, 102, 103-110
Expressionism, 17
Extramarital relations, 4, 120-121,
    144
    Kinsey Report on, 62
    19th century double standard
        for men vs. women, 9-10

"Facts of life," 52, 145
Fads, and fetishism, 110-111
Family:
> changes of male and female roles in, 89-90, 91, 120, 124-129
> disintegration, as cause of homosexuality, 86-88, 95
> nuclear, problems of survival of, 130-131
> sex education in, 119-124, 144-145

Fashions, sexual symbolism in, 3, 110
"Father Knows Best" (TV show), 126
Father role, 89, 90, 91, 120, 124-129, 141
Father-son relationship, 126-128
> and homosexuality, 90, 91, 96-97
> show of tenderness in, 127-128

Feingold, Michael, 134-135
Female role, 140-143
> double standard of morality, 9, 10, 12, 23, 133
> in the family, 89-90, 120, 124, 125, 126, 127

Female sexuality, changing view of, 140-143
Femininity, 5, 46, 97, 141
> passivity association, 78

*Femme de Paul, La* (Maupassant), 14
Fetishism, 3, 24, 28, 50, 72, 101-111
> "anthropologic" theory of, 109-110
> Binet's association theory of, 107-108
> case history, 102-110
> cultural aspects of, 110-111
> and fads, 3, 110-111

fetish as motherly phallus, 107-109
Freudian view of, 101, 107-108, 109
gestalt theory of fetish, 109
of homosexuals, 108-109, 110
mass media depiction of, 137
normal vs. abnormal (Becker), 101-102
orthodox interpretation of, 101
phallic vs. nonphallic meaning of fetishes, 108-109
rarity in women, 109
therapy of, 102, 103-110
uniforms and, 73

"Fetishism" (Freud), 50
*First and the Last, The* (Galsworthy), 13
Flagellation, 17, 70, 72, 73
Flaubert, Gustave:
> *Madame Bovary,* 137
> *L'Education sentimentale,* 135

*Fliegende Blätter* (humor magazine), 13
Fliess, Wilhelm, 75-76
Flogging, 70, 72
Forel, André, 12, 23, 26-27
France, 17
> low rate of homosexuality, 127n.
> syphilis, 72

Fraternity initiation rites, 71
Free love:
> early exponents of, 11
> emergence of wide discussion of, around 1900, 13, 38-39
> *See also* Sexual freedom

Freud, Anna, 49
Freud, Sigmund, 1, 2, 3, 14, 26, 28,

42-54, 80, 135, 140
"Analysis Terminable and Interminable," 78-79
and bisexuality, 75-76, 77-79, 80
"A Child is Being Beaten," 50, 113
"A Contribution on the Study of the Origin of Sexual Perversions," 50
early reaction to, by medical profession, 38
"The Economic Problem of Masochism," 50
emphasis on sexual instinct, 43, 51
essay on Leonardo, 28
and fetishism, 101, 107, 108, 109
"Fetishism," 50
and Havelock Ellis, 34-35
*The Interpretation of Dreams,* 38, 42
*New Introductory Lectures,* 78
quoted, on delineation of perversion, 67-68
quoted, on sadism, 112
quoted, on sexual enlightenment, 52
*Studies in Hysteria,* 55
*Three Contributions to the Theory of Sex,* 4, 42-43, 44, 48, 52, 55
view of homosexuality, 50-51
view of masochism, 113
view of sexual liberation, 53
Freudian theory, 42, 44-51, 59
concept of bisexuality in, 75-76, 77-78, 79, 80

influence on sexual liberation, 55
of libido, 43, 47, 50
modifications, 47-51 (*see also* Neo-Freudians; Post-Freudians)
"orthodox," 49
of psychosexual development, 43, 46-47, 50, 55, 57
relevancy today, 46-47
U. S. reaction and approach to, 44-49, 55
view of fetishism, 101, 107-108, 109
Friedenberg, Edgar, 95
Friedman, Alan, 138
Frigidity, 28, 46, 94, 109
Fromm, Erich, 49
Fryer, Peter, 33
*Futurist Manifesto of Lust* (Saint Point), 137

Galsworthy, John, 13
Gebsattel, V. E. von, 60, 104, 109
Genet, Jean, 3, 137
George IV, King of England, 72
Germany:
homosexuality, 17, 18-22, 72-73, 135
Imperial (pre-World War I) era, 16-18, 23, 72, 73, 135
pioneering in sexology, 23, 25-29, 35
sexology of present, 60
Wilhelm II's Court camarilla of Urnings, 18-22
*Geschlecht und Charakter* (Weininger), 14
*Geschlechtskunde* (Hirschfeld), 25-26

*Geschlechtsleben der Erwachsenen* (Hirschfeld), 26
Gestalt theory, and fetishes, 109
*Ghosts* (Ibsen), 135
Gide, André, 80, 85
Giese, Hans, 60, 92
Gillespie, W. H., 68
"Girl Friends" (Courbet), 136
Girl Guides, 40
Gley, E., 75
Goethe, Johann Wolfgang von, 13, 28, 134
Gogh, Vincent van, 28
Goodman, Paul, 45-46, 95
Gorer, Geoffrey, 115
Great Depression, 41
Greece, ancient homosexuality in, 57
*Growing Up Absurd* (Goodman), 46
Guyon, René, 137

Hall, G. Stanley, 45
*Handbook for Girl Guides, A* (Baden Powell), 40
*Hanneles Himmelfahrt* (Hauptmann), 16
*Hans Brinker* (Leland), 137
Harden, Maximilian, 19-22
Hartmann, Karl Robert von, 49
Heidegger, Martin, 105, 106
*Henri Brulard, Life of* (Stendhal), 43-44, 135
Herman, G., 76
Hermaphroditism, 138
    physical, and bisexuality, 76-77
Hirschfeld, Magnus, 23, 24, 25-26, 27-28, 60, 61, 62, 145
    and bisexuality, 77
    and fetishism, 72, 101
    and sadomasochism, 72, 112

*Sexual Anomalies and Perversions*, 50
    studies of homosexuality, 25, 27, 74
    writings of, 25-26, 72
Hitler, Adolf, 26, 73
Hitschmann, Eduard, 28, 52
Hofmannsthal, Hugo von, 28
Hohenlohe-Schillingfurst, Prince Chlodwig zu, 16
Holstein, Friedrich von, 21
*Homogenic Love* (Carpenter), 39
*Homosexualität des Mannes und des Weibes, Die* (Hirschfeld), 25
Homosexuality, 4, 75, 82-100, 122, 134, 143
    Bieber's study, 50, 96
    Carpenter's defense of, 33, 38-39
    castrating mother as cause of, 90, 96-97
    "catamites," 19
    causes of, 87, 90-91, 95, 96-97, 100
    as cogenital condition, 39
    covert, 93
    as a crime, 17-18, 21-22, 27, 33, 37, 82
    cultural genesis of, 50
    ease of finding partners, 90
    Ellis's studies of, 36, 37, 74
    family disorganization as cause of, 86-90, 95
    fetishism in, 108-109, 110
    Freud's views of, 50-51, 57
    in Germany, 17-23, 72-73, 135
    Hirschfeld's studies of, 25, 27, 74
    incidental experiences of

heterosexuals, 90-91
increase in U.S., 83, 85, 86-88, 92-93
Kinsey on, 56-57
Krafft-Ebing's studies, 74, 77
lack of sociological studies on, 49, 74, 83
latent, 78-79, 93
in literature, 14, 80, 85-86
low rate in France, 127n.
and married life, 79-80, 81, 83, 143n.
mass media depiction of, 137
and myth of bisexuality, 75-76, 77, 78-81
as natural form of human behavior, 36, 39, 69
among Nazis, 73
and neurosis, 83-84, 91
normal among Korakis and Big Nambas, 69
opportunities for developing, 92-93, 96
overt, 93-95
as a personality problem, 84-85, 96-100
in prison, 82, 97
public attitudes, 40-41, 82, 83
sadomasochism in, 110
sanctioned by Plains Indians, 71
as a social phenomenon, 86, 92, 95-96
state laws on, 82
stereotypic notions of, 83-84, 97
therapy of, 73, 85, 91, 96, 99
"the third sex," 27
three types of homosexuals, 93-95

"Uranians," 38
Urnings, 18-22
Wilde's case, 9, 10, 21
among women, 85-86 (*see also* Lesbianism)
Hooker, Evelyn, 84
Howells, William Dean, 125
Huysmans, Joris Karl, 34
Hysteria, 52

Ibsen, Henrik, 34, 135
Impotence, 28, 103, 143
increase in, 125
*Impressions and Comments* (Ellis), 34
Incest, movie depiction of, 137
Incest complex, 104-105
Infantile sexuality, 43-44, 45, 48
and fetishism, 107-108
in neurotics, 43, 49
its role de-emphasized in newer psychoanalytic schools, 49
Ingres, Jean Auguste Dominique, 136
Initiation rites, 71
"Inquest on Love," 137
Institute of Sexual Science, Berlin, 25-26
*Intermediate Sex, The* (Carpenter), 39
*Interpretation of Dreams, The* (Freud), 38, 42
Inversion, sexual, 50, 75-76. *See also* Homosexuality

Jews, frequency of neurotic ailments, 52
Jones, Ernest, 43
Judeo-Christian morality, 69-71, 133, 139
Jung, Carl Gustav, 42, 53-54, 135

*Kangacreek* (Ellis), 34
Kardiner, Abram, 90
Keller, Gottfried, 28
Keniston, Kenneth, 126
Kielholz, Arthur, 28
Kinsey, Alfred C., 1, 4, 55-59, 60, 62, 69, 80
Kinsey Institute, 57, 58, 59
Kinsey Reports, 50, 56-57, 61
Klein, Melanie, 68
Kleist, Heinrich von, 28
Kollwitz, Käthe, 16
Korakis, 69
Krafft-Ebing, Richard, 23, 24, 26, 27, 55, 60, 61, 62, 71-72, 135, 145
    and bisexuality, 76, 77
    and fetishism, 72, 101
    and homosexuality, 74, 77
    *Psychopathia Sexualis,* 26, 36, 50, 72
    and sadomasochism, 72, 112
    technical language used by, 36
Kris, Ernst, 75
Kunz, H., 109

*Lady of the Camelias* (Dumas), 135
La Guardia, Fiorello, 124
*Lancet, The* (medical journal), 37
"Latent Homosexuality" (Salzman), 79
Lees, Edith (Mrs. Havelock Ellis), 33
*Leisure and Pleasure in the Nineteenth Century* (Margetson), 31
Leland, Charles, 137
Lenau, Nikolaus, 28
Leonardo da Vinci, 28
Leopold I, King of Belgium, 2, 31
Lesbianism, 14, 33, 85-86, 94
    mass media depiction of, 137

Libido, Freudian theory, 43, 47, 50
*Libido Sexualis* (Moll), 27
*Liebelei* (Schnitzler), 13
*Lieder,* expression of sexuality in, 134
*Life of Henri Brulard* (Stendhal), 43-44, 135
Lillie, F. R., 78
Literature, expression of sexuality in, 13, 28, 34, 43-44, 134, 135-136, 137-138
    bisexuality, 80
    homosexuality, 14, 80, 85
    Lesbianism, 85-86
    masturbation, 138
    sadomasochism, 112-113, 114, 115
Lombroso, Cesare, 135
*Lonely Crowd, The* (Riesman), 130
Longford, Elisabeth, 30
Longworth, Alice Roosevelt, 44
Lorand, Sandor, 101
Louis XIV, King of France, 20
Louise, Queen of Belgium, 2
Lowenstein, Prince, 31
"Lunch on the Grass" (Manet), 136
Lyttelton, Edward, 39-40

"Mad Love" (Breton), 137
"Mad Nudists," 12
*Madame Bovary* (Flaubert), 137
Magic, 69, 70
*Maisons de tolerance,* 10
Male role:
    activity association, 78
    in the family, 89, 90, 91, 120, 124-129, 141
    and modern vocations, 88-89
    at work, 127, 129
    *See also* Masculinity

Manet, Edouard, 136
Mann, Heinrich, 17
Mansfield, Jayne, 136
Mansour, Joyce, 137
Mantegazza, Paolo, 12
Maranon, M., 137
Marcus, Steven, 31-32
Margetson, Stella, 31
Marie, Grand Duchess of Russia, 30
Marriage, 4, 39-40, 63, 129, 130, 133, 134, 140, 141, 144
    committees on reform of (early 1900's), 13
    dissatisfaction with, 142-144, 146
    dual morality for women vs. men, 19th century, 10
    heterosexual, of homosexuals, 79-80, 81, 93
    intercourse, 130
    partner swapping, 130
    trial, 13, 130
    See also Extramarital relations; Family
Marriage in a Free Society (Carpenter), 38
Martin, Theodore, 12
Masculinity, 5, 46, 97, 128
    activity association, 78
    as a front, 143
    See also Male role
Masochism, 50, 73, 113. See also Sadomasochism
Mass media:
    depiction of father in, 125-126
    exploitation of sex by, 134, 137-138
Masters and Johnson, study of human sexual response, 56

Masturbation, 32, 52, 84, 124, 133
    film and literary treatment of, 137, 138
    Freud and, 52, 57
    Kinsey as source of data on, 62
Maternity, 140-141. See also Mother role
Maupassant, Guy de, 14
Maurice, F. D., 38
Mehring, Walter, 17
Men:
    aggression factor in sexuality of, 112
    19th century sexual morality for, 9-10
    See also Father role; Male role; Masculinity
Merleau-Ponty, Maurice, 139
Middle Ages, 132-133
    childhood, 131
    homosexuality, 72
    prostitution, 10, 133
    restrictions on sex, 121, 132-133
    self-flagellation, 70
Military life, 73
Miller, Henry, 3, 136
Miller, Milton, 80
Mistresses, of 19th century, 10, 130n.
Mobius, P. G., 14
Moll, Albert, 23, 27
    The Sexual Life of the Child, 51-52
Moltke, Kuno von, Count, 22
Money-semen analogy, Victorian era, 32
Mother role, 89-90, 120, 124, 125, 126, 127, 140-141
Mother-child relationship, 43, 107,

124, 126
Mother-son relationship:
  and fetishism, 102-109
  and homosexuality, 90, 96-97
  infant sexuality, 43-44
"Mourning rings," 71
Movies, display of sexuality in, 137
Muensterberger, Warner, 68, 69
*My Secret Life* (anon.), 31

Napoleonic Code, 10, 59
Narcissism, 57, 69
Naturalism, influence on sexual
  mores, 11
Nazism, 72, 73
Necromancy, 70
Neo-Freudians, 47, 59, 81, 101
Neurosis, 43, 96, 126
  bisexuality and, 76, 80
  causes of, 68, 132-133
  dynamics of, 49
  homosexuality and, 83-84, 91
  among Jews, 52
  role of infantile sexuality in, 43,
    49
New Guinea, Korakis of, 69
New Hebrides, Big Nambas of, 69
*New Introductory Lectures* (Freud), 78
New York City, Academy of
  Medicine, 26
Newspapers, 134, 137
Nietzsche, Friedrich Wilhelm, 14, 28
Normality vs. abnormality, sexual,
  67-74
  author's terminology, 67n.
  biological criterion for, 68
  cultural criteria for, 57, 60, 67,
    69
  emphasis misplaced, 63, 69

Freud on line between, 67-68
individual criteria for, 52, 69
moralistic criteria of, continuing emphasis, 59-60
Novels. *See* Literature

Oedipus complex, 105-106
*120 Days of Sodom* (de Sade), 112,
  115
Oral stage of development, ego splitting, 68
Orgasm, relative importance, in advanced vs. simple society, 46
*Origins of Psychoanalysis, The* (Kris),
  75-76
*Other Victorians, The* (Marcus), 31

Painting, 19th century prudery toward,
  136
Pan-sexuality, 57
Parenthood, 131, 141
  and sex education, 119-124,
    144-145
  *See also* Family; Father role;
    Father-son relationship;
    Mother role; Mother-child
    relationship; Mother-son re-
    lationship
Paris, 136, 137
  committee on marriage reform
    (1906), 13
Parnell, Charles Stewart, 10
Partner swapping, 130
Pathology, sexual, 24, 26, 27, 55, 145
  continued European emphasis
    on, 60, 62
Pathography, 28
Perversion, sexual, 17, 24, 52, 67-74,
  134, 140

"anthropologic" theory of, 109
author's terminology, 67n.
Binet's association theory of, 107-108
causes of, 68, 132
definition by biological criterion, 68
definition by cultural criteria, 57, 60, 67, 69
definition by individual criteria, 52, 69
early studies of, 25, 26, 27-28, 36, 37, 39, 74
Freud quoted, 67-68
Freud's writings on, 50
ignorance widespread and continuing, 48
and Judeo-Christian morality, 69-71
lack of contemporary studies of, 73-74
moralist concepts of, 59-60
the "other sexuality" (Scheler), 60
See also Fetishism; Flagellation; Homosexuality; Masochism; Sadism; Sadomasochism; Transvestism
Phallic stage of development, ego splitting, 68
Photography, 136
"art," 12
Plains Indians, 71
Pleasure (underground newspaper), 143n.
Plotinus, 70
Poetry, expression of sexuality in, 134, 137
Pornography, 124, 136, 145-146

censorship of, 33, 124
customers of, 142
sadistic, 113
in Victorian England, 30, 31, 32-33
Portnoy's Complaint (Roth), 138
Post-Freudians, 49, 101
Pregenital sexual drive and expression, 68, 69, 72, 73
Premarital sex, 62, 120-121
Primal anxiety, 105, 106-107
Pritchett, V. S., 11
Prostitution, 146
Middle Ages, 10, 133
19th century, 9-10, 23, 32, 123, 135, 136
Proust, Marcel, 14, 80, 85
Psychiatry, 19th century, 24
Psychoanalysis, 28, 42, 47, 59, 85
classical, 4, 101
clinical, 38
concept of bisexuality in, 75-76, 77-78, 79, 80
continued use of moralistic sexual criteria, 59-60
culturalist school, 49, 50, 51
existentialist school, 47, 49, 60, 79, 92, 102, 103-110
familiarity of terms of, 98
influence on sexual liberation, 55
post-Freudian, 48, 49-51
Sartre on, 47-48
See also Psychotherapy
Psychoanalytic Society of Berlin, 26
Psychoanalytic Society of Vienna, 51-54
Psychology of Sex, The (Ellis), 34-35, 36-37, 50, 61

*Psychopathia Sexualis* (Krafft-Ebing), 26, 36, 50, 72
Psychosexual development, Freudian theory of, 43, 46-47, 50, 55, 57
   Kinsey's view, 57-58
   oral-phallic ego splitting in, and perversion, 68
Psychosis:
   anxiety, 106
   vs. sexual perversion, 68
Psychotherapy, 49-50
   bisexuality rejected in, 79, 80
   client-centered, Rogers, 48
   existentialist school of, 47, 49, 79, 92, 102, 103-110
   of fetishists, 102, 103-110
   of homosexuals, 85, 91, 96, 99
   *See also* Psychoanalysis
Puberty, 45
   declining age of, 142
Puritanism, vestiges of, 55, 59, 144
Putnam, James, 48

Radio, 134, 137
Rado, Sandor, 76-78
Rank, Otto, 42
Reage, Pauline, 137
*Recherche du temps perdu, A la* (Proust), 14
*Reigen* (Schnitzler), 13
Repression of sex drive, 32-33, 123, 132-133, 139
Ricoeur, Paul, 62-63, 119, 122
Rieff, Philip, 85
Riesman, David, 130, 141-142
Rilke, Rainer Maria, 14
*Rise of Silas Lapham* (Howells), 125
Roehm, Ernst, 73
Rogers, Carl, 48

Roosevelt, Theodore, 44
*Rosenkavalier* (Strauss), 16
Rostow, Edna, 143
Rousseau, Jean Jacques, 28

Sacher-Masoch, Leopold von, 70, 113
Sade, Marquis de, 70, 112, 113-116, 136
Sadger, Isidor, 23, 27, 28, 52
Sadism, 28, 50, 73, 112-116
   Freud quoted on, 112
   mass media depiction of, 137
   normal among Korakis and Big Nambas, 69
Sadistic pornography, 113
Sadomasochism, 17, 24, 70, 72, 73, 112-116
   in homosexuals, 110
   "le vice Anglais," 17, 72
Saint Point, Valentine de, 137
*Salome* (Strauss), 16
Salzman, Leon, 79
Sartre, Jean-Paul, 47, 115
Scheler, Max, 60
Schelsky, Helmut, 60, 88
Schick, Alfred, 51
Schiller, Friedrich von, 28
Schnitzler, Arthur, 13, 28
Schubert, Franz, 134
Schulenburg, Count Günther von der, 20
*Secret Life, My* (anon.), 31
Self-flagellation, 70
Semen-money analogy, Victorian era, 32
*Sex and Character* (Weininger), 14, 76
*Sex and Society* (Ellis), 12
Sex education, 11, 119-124, 144-145

discussion of, at Vienna Psychoanalytical Society (1908), 52

in the schools, 120

*Sex-love and its place in a Free Society* (Carpenter), 38

Sex Research Institute, University of Indiana, 55

*Sexual Aberrations* (Stekel), 101

*Sexual Anomalies and Perversions* (Hirschfeld), 50

Sexual freedom, 11, 13, 38-39, 53-54, 142-146

*Sexual Inversion* (Ellis), 37

*Sexual Life of the Child, The* (Moll), 52

*Sexual Problem, The* (Forel), 12, 27

Sexual revolution, 2, 124

Sexual role, male versus female, 5, 51, 78, 88-89, 124-126, 127-128

adolescent pressures, 45-46, 90

sociological changes in, 88-89, 140-143

*See also* Female role; Male role

*Sexualleben unserer Zeit, Das* (Bloch), 12

*Sexuelle Frage, Die* (Forel), 12, 27

*Sexuelle Neuropathie* (Sadger), 27

*Sexuelle Not, Die* (Wittels), 52-54

Shakespeare, William, 133

Shaw, George Bernard, 12

*Silver Skates, The* (Leland), 137

*Simplizissimus* (humor magazine), 27

"Sin," 9-10, 13

*Sister Carrie* (Dreiser), 137

Smiles, Samuel, 32

Socialism, 38

influence on sexual mores, 11, 41

*Sociology of Sexuality* (Schelsky), 60

Sodomy, mass media depiction of, 137

*Soul of Spain, The* (Ellis), 34

*Soziologie der Sexualität* (Schelsky), 60

SS, Nazi elite guard, 73

State laws, on homosexuality, 82

Stauffer, Karl, 28

Stekel, Wilhelm, 23, 28, 101

Stendhal (*pseudonym of* Marie Henri Beyle), 43-44, 135

Sternheim, Carl, 17

Stimuli, role in sexual development, 57-58

Stockmar, Baron Christian Friedrich von, 31

*Story of O, The* (Reage), 113

Straus, E., 109

Strauss, Richard, 16, 28

Strindberg, August, 14

*Studies in Hysteria* (Freud and Breuer), 55

*Studies of the Psychology of Sex* (Ellis), 34-35, 36-37, 50, 61

Surrealism, 137

Swinburne, Algernon Charles, 34, 72, 136

Symbolism, sexual, 3, 110

Symonds, John Addington, 79-80

Syphilis, 72

Taylor, Rattray, 132, 133

Television, 134, 137

depiction of father on, 125-126

*See also* Advertising

Tennyson, Alfred, Lord, 136

Theater, sexual display in, 134-135, 137

Thoreau, Henry David, 63

*Three Contributions to the Theory of Sex* (Freud), 4, 42-43, 44, 48, 52, 55
*Thrift* (Smiles), 32
Thurber, James, 133
*Times* (of London), 40
*Training of the Young in the Law of Sex, The* (Lyttelton), 40
Transvestism, 24, 71
Trial marriage, 13, 130
*Tropic of Cancer* (Miller), 136
Tschudi, Hugo von, 16
"Turkish Bath" (Ingres), 136

Ullerstam, Lars, 3
Ulrichs, Karl Heinrich, 18n.
Underwear, feminine, as fetish, 108
Uniforms, fetishistic appeal of, 73
United States:
    father role, compared to European father, 126-127
    and Freudian theory, 44-49, 55
    increase of homosexuality, 83, 85, 86-88, 92-93
    Kinsey's influence, 55-56, 58-59, 61
    vestiges of Puritanism in, 55, 59
    women of, compared with European women, 89
University of Indiana, Sex Research Institute, 55
"Uranians," 38
*Uranlage,* 77
Urnings, 18-22
Urogenital system, embryonic development of, 76-77, 78

Van Gogh, Vincent, 28
Van Kaam, Adrian, 139

Venereal disease, 17, 24, 32
    fight against, complicated by condemnation of VD, 53
    prostitution and, 10
*Venus in Furs* (Sacher-Masoch), 113
Victoria, Queen of England, 30-31, 34
*Victoria R. I.* (Longford), 30
Victorian era, 30-33, 136
    family of, 120, 140
    "innocent" childhood, 43, 120, 145
    money-semen analogy, 32
    morality of, 9-12, 30, 31-33, 123, 135, 140
    pornography, 30, 31, 32-33
    prostitution, 9-10, 32, 123, 135
    sexology, 33-39
Vidal, Gore, 85
Vienna:
    committee on marriage reform (1906), 13
    Freudian, 51-54
    Psychoanalytic Society, 51-54
Vizetelly, Henry, 33
Vorberg, Gaston, 28

Watch and Ward Society of Boston, 135
*Way of all Flesh, The* (Butler), 11
Wedekind, Franz, 17
Weimar, Poets Monument of, 27-28
Weininger, Otto, 14, 76
Wellington, Duke of, 31
Wettley, Annemarie, 60
"White slave" traffic, 135
Wilde, Oscar, 9, 10, 21, 30, 80, 135
Wilhelm II, Kaiser, 16, 18-22, 23, 73, 135
*Willy-Nilly* (Friedman), 138

Wittels, Fritz, 52-54
Wolf, Hugo, 28
Wolfenden Report, 39
*Woman and her place in a Free Society*
    (Carpenter), 39
Women:
    change of role of, in modern
      America, 89-90, 140-142
      (*see also* Mother role)
    changing view of sexuality of,
      140-143
    double standard of morals for,
      9, 10, 23, 133, 135
    emancipation of, 11, 14, 40-41
    homosexuality among, 85-86
      (*see also* Lesbianism)

19th century sexual morality
    for, 9, 10, 12
orgasm, 46
rarity of fetishism in, 109
sexual satisfaction, 140-141
    *See also* Female role; Feminin-
      ity
Women's suffrage, 14
World War I, 25, 40, 55, 136
World War II, 60
Wortis, Joseph, 35

Youth movements, 40, 72-73, 91

*Zukunft, Die* (magazine), 18-19, 21

Dr. Hendrik Ruitenbeek is the author of many distinguished books dealing with human sexuality and with the theories of Dr. Sigmund Freud. His other books include *Sexuality and Identity, Freud and America,* and *Heirs to Freud.*